Journey from Ignorance to Self-Awareness

A brief memoir of abuse, support and achievement

Patrick Shen

2022

Contents

Part 1 – My memoir as told via a factual narrative 6

  Preface 6

  About me 9

  Early Life (pre-twelve) 11

    Aggressive Behaviours 11

    Chores and Responsibilities 15

    Silent Abuse - Verbal, Emotional and Physical 19

    Low Income Family and our Neighbours 32

    Strength in Academic Pursuit and Sporting Achievements 37

    Early signs of an ASD brain 39

    Ignorance and Sarcasm 41

    First Signs of Mental Illness, Misdiagnosed, and then Ignored by Parents 44

    Unknown Support Person 46

    James and My Loss of Memory Pre-Twelve 48

  12-15-year-old 52

    First Paid jobs 52

    High School Achievements and Supportive People 54

    Change of Towns 57

  15-19 63

    Parent's Divorce and Parental Engagement 63

    First Love 66

From North Queensland to Brisbane and Back 68

Second Love 74

Signs of My Mental Illness 77

Realisation and Appreciation of My Sister and Improved Relationship 82

NQ Martial Arts as Self-Medication 84

19 + ... 86

More Focus on My Future Wife 86

Healing Begins 89

Study, Work and Mental Illness 91

Family History of Mental Illness and Trauma 98

Memory and Processing Today 102

Being a Psychologist with ASD and PTSD 107

Identifying Positives thus far 111

Looking towards the future 116

Barriers only slow us down 116

My Parenting 123

Moving Forward 127

Various Discriminations 131

Memoir Close 134

Part 2 – My Memoir as told via a factual but artistic lens (poem) 135

Preface 135

About Me 136

Aggressive Behaviours 138

Chores and Responsibilities 140

Silent Abuse – Verbal, Emotional and Physical 142

Low Income Family and our Neighbours 148

Strength in Academic Pursuit and Sporting Achievements 151

Early signs of an ASD brain 152

Ignorance and Sarcasm 153

First Signs of Mental Illness, Misdiagnosed, and then Ignored by Parents 155

James and My Loss of Memory Pre-Twelve 157

First Paid Jobs 160

Change of Towns 162

Parent's Divorce and Parental Engagement 165

First Love 167

From North Queensland to Brisbane and Back 168

Second Love 173

Signs of My Mental Illness 175

Realisation and Appreciation of My Sister and Improved Relationship 179

NQ Martial Arts as Self-Medication 180

More Focus on My Future Wife 182

Healing Begins 183

Study, Work and Mental Illness 185

Family History of Mental Illness and Trauma 189

Memory and Processing Today 191

Being a Psychologist with ASD and PTSD 193

Identifying Positive thus far 195

Barriers only slow us down 197

My Parenting 201

Moving Forward 203

Various Discriminations 205

Memoir Close 208

Appendix 210

Part 1 – My memoir as told via a factual narrative

Preface

During my time volunteering for a community mental health organisation, I was told that the sharing of my story to high school students and university students was able to help some of the young people who heard it. Following the presentation of my story, young people would often ask me questions about my experience of having Autism (ASD) or Post-Traumatic Stress Disorder (PTSD) and how I managed to cope. Before leaving the organisation, I was filmed sharing my story, so that the organisation could use it to show high school children, when I could not make the presentation days.

During my experience as a psychologist, many young people have expressed to me their own stories of trauma and how they felt they were alone in their experience. It is my hope that this brief memoir can assist people to understand there are various ways to get through life's challenges, and if you are lucky enough, learn some valuable life lessons.

The title of this book 'Ignorance to Self-Awareness' was chosen as I believe that my ignorance regarding the negatives of my childhood were once a protective and a positive factor for me. However, I now believe that my eventual self-awareness became my biggest ally in being able to identify warning signs and symptoms of my mental illness which has helped me make better behavioural choices. As I will discuss later in the memoir, I am very logical, so my story will be told as more matter of fact than emotional journey. However, I have attempted to express more of my own personal emotions where appropriate, which is something that does not come easy for me. I feel that my logical interpretation of the world may stem in part from my childhood environment, but also comes from my diagnosed Autism.

In the process of writing this, I have had to ask several friends and colleagues about how someone with my symptoms of ASD and PTSD can write about emotion. The response often provided was, for me to highlight this weakness to assist, you the reader, to understand my difficulties more accurately.

The names in the book, including my own, have been changed for anonymity, to protect some of the people in my memoir. My name was changed to protect my future career prospects. I have unfortunately witnessed that there is still stigma in the mental health field and medical field as a whole. Whilst I want this memoir to be able to help others, I feel that I am not yet in a strong enough position professionally to risk losing my job, which would impact my own family.

I would like to say thank you to my sister, my friend James, other friends including Pat and Charles, and my wife who assisted in writing this memoir. I would also like to say a special thank you to my sister, James, Mat and his family, Margaret and her family and my wife for supporting me through my many struggles and allowing me to become the best version of myself.

I asked my sister to draw the cover for the memoir as her drawing ability is much greater than my own. The tree represents growth and the Penrose Staircase represents the ongoing work a person needs to do for their mental health. I added the different colours to represent emotions and demonstrate that all of our emotions are part of our recovery journey.

About me

I was born in the late 1980's in Mackay, QLD. I spent most of my childhood in a small country town near Brisbane, where I lived with my mother, father, and younger sister. Despite my family working hard, we were what would be considered low-income family. When my parents sold our two-storey house of ten years and my father injured his back, they had just enough money left over for us to travel to our new location to live, where we would move in with my aunty.

I cannot remember my first twelve years of existence, and as such, any stories I share throughout the book that happened during this time have been told to me by my sister, parents, or close friends. As I will discuss later, I have a poor interpersonal memory in general and unfortunately can remember when people wrong me, but have great difficulty remembering positive events such as the birth of children. Occasionally I have what could be considered an emotional-muscle memory (somatic) where I don't know why, but I have a strong positive or often negative emotional reaction to neutral stimuli. The few occasions I have discussed this with one of my supportive people, they have been able to fill in the memory details for me.

I have had various behavioural issues, mostly involving anger, that continue to impact me today. I experienced various forms of abuse over a fifteen-year period, that may have shaped me, but I do not let that define me. I have met people who I identify as supports and positive role models from my childhood through to today. I feel I have learnt valuable life lessons about people and the world, and I was able to overcome life's adversities.

Despite the many negative events, outcomes and effects that are discussed in this memoir, I feel I was fortunate in many ways, which I will discuss later. I am grateful for the many life lessons I have learnt along my journey, as I feel I have had an advantage over some of my peers due to having to learn about the world at a younger age.

I currently work full time as a psychologist, own a small personal training, group fitness and Pilate's business, have a supportive family; and continue to be in contact with the people who have helped shape me for the better.

Early Life (pre-twelve)

<u>Aggressive Behaviours</u>

During my primary school years, I was physically destructive and aggressive towards other students, and property at home (when I was six, I punched a hole through my bedroom door in anger). I was bullied during years one and two at my first primary school; and when bullied would often respond with aggression. I once slammed an older student into a metal water bubbler headfirst, for teasing me. Due to this bullying and behaviour, I was forced to change primary schools.

At my new primary school, I was bullied again for the next two years. In one example of aggressive retaliation, I threw a senior student down a flight of stairs for teasing me, and my parents had to be called to the school as the teachers found it difficult to remove me from the larger student. Another example where I was the victim of school bullying involved three of my peers in grade four. These bullies attacked me during a lunch break when I refused to do what they wanted me to do. The bullies received no punishment for attacking me, as one of the bullies had a parent at the school who was a teacher, and another had a parent whose father was the local police officer and whose mother was involved with the school board. The third student who went unpunished by the school, chose to bully me several days later in retaliation for me telling my parents about the previous event. Following this second lot of bullying by the same student, he was punished by being banned from playing soccer during school breaks for only a month.

When my parents asked me what punishment the three children received for attacking at school, I lied and told them that they collectively were not allowed to play school sport. I did this as I felt that if I told my parents the truth, I would receive more bullying at school from my peers. Upon hearing about the soccer punishment, my parents insulted me for being weak and threatened not to help me again if I was bullied and didn't stand up for myself, because somehow, they thought the school's decision was my fault.

Due to this bullying and behaviour, it appeared that I was going to change schools again; but was allowed to continue my schooling because the only two public schools in the area merged. From years five to seven I was bullied again, sometimes beaten by groups of children, both at school and on the way home from school.

The most extreme incident involved me being hung headfirst over a bridge by the neighbour's children. The bridge incident happened a week after I refused to share my property with the neighbour's kids, at a social gathering. I wore a motorcycle helmet with my bicycle as that was the only helmet, we had available at home at the time, and when I arrived at the social gathering two of the kids there wanted the helmet. I refused to share it as I was given explicit instructions by my parents to not let anyone touch the helmet. Following my refusal, the two kids waited for me to walk home from school one afternoon, and then when they saw me, they threatened me by hanging me over a bridge (which was above a set of railway lines). When I returned home that afternoon, I told my mother, and she had a "conversation" with the two kid's guardian and walked me home for several days following. Thankfully, they did not bother me again.

Unsurprisingly to many people in my town, my mother had a reputation for being aggressive towards teachers when I was bullied or wronged at school. One such incident involved a photo I brought to school in year four, getting accidently damaged by water. When my mother saw the water damaged photo, she became very angry at the teacher for not doing a better job of protecting my property and went to the school to "sort it out". When she arrived at the school angry, the principal escorted the teacher out of school grounds because of my mother's reputation (of being overly aggressive) while the deputy principal attempted to resolve the situation.

Until I was approximately ten, I was also aggressive towards my sister; she was two years younger and smaller and became an easy target for my anger and frustration. One time, during a family road trip, I responded to a verbal argument by sitting on top of my sister and punching her continuously, which forced my parents to stop and pullover; where they would then go on to physically punish me.

My aggressive behaviour, and aggressive reactions to peers and my sister may have been the early warning signs of trauma combined with the learnt behaviours demonstrated by my parents. However, due to living in a small country town with no communication about mental health or abuse, I now understand why no one did anything to stop my parent's behaviours.

Chores and Responsibilities

In my household, chores were a regular part of life. By the age of five, my mornings consisted of feeding our two dogs and any other animals we had (fish, guinea pigs, etc.), preparing my school lunch, cleaning my room, and then getting ready for school. If my school lunch was not up to my mother's standards, physical punishment ensued. With the most ridiculous example involving how I cut my sandwich. I cut my sandwich into random shapes for fun, as it was for myself, but when my mother saw this, I received a physical punishment and had to redo my lunch.

My nights often involved washing the family's dishes before I was allowed to go to sleep. Some nights, this was not finished until 10pm as I would try to avoid the dishes or not do them to my mother's standard and would often receive various punishments for this. The weekends included cleaning the dog's mess in the yard, mowing (when I was older), and any other required tasks needed around the house. Resentment towards my sister may have started when I was around seven years of age.

Even though I had asthma and used an asthma machine known as a Nebuliser, once or twice a week, my sister had worse asthma than me. This meant she was on a Nebuliser daily, had almost no chores, and often was not required to make her own bed until she was about eleven. Through the eyes of a child, this felt like I was doing everything, and felt like my sister was doing nothing. As an adult I have come to realise that the resentment I had towards my sister as a child, has also manifested in the way I see other adults. If I perceive someone in my personal life is not "pulling their weight", I can become easily triggered and begin focusing on their flaws. However, once I realise this, I then attempt to communicate and resolve my feelings.

When I was younger my mother had an operation. Due to my mother's declining leg health relating to varicose veins, she needed to have both of her legs operated on at the same time and apparently had a fifty percent chance of survival. The leg operation meant she was unable to walk for several weeks and was unable to walk well for several months. During this period, my father was away for work often and this meant that the family's grocery shopping became my responsibility. So, at around age twelve, I would ride to the shops on my BMX with cash and a list and get the fortnight-month's grocery shopping. I would then carry the shopping on my bike and ride home. I have since been reminded on various occasions by my former German subject teacher Margaret, that she had seen me balancing the grocery shopping on the handlebars and riding with the larger items such as ten kilograms of potatoes, on my knees while heading home.

Growing up in a small country town, sometimes meant assisting my father with cleaning the septic tank, or often moving the full compost garbage bin to the backyard compost pile. On one occasion due to the garbage bin being completely full, and therefore too heavy for my twelve-year-old self, I lost control and the contents from the bin landed onto my body, covering me in compost. After getting into trouble for being impatient and not moving the compost bin correctly, my parents showered me and removed as much of the compost smell as they could. However, the bin falling on me, meant that I smelled of compost for a whole week. Thankfully, I did not have any long-term injuries.

The many chores and responsibilities were seen as normal to me, and I feel led to a strong work ethic in my adult years. Many people who know me as an adult today often remark "my parents did a good job raising me", framing my current work ethic as my parents' doing. However, for me this comment often silently triggers the many negative emotions I have because of the types of punishments I received as a child and how I was parented in general.

Silent Abuse - Verbal, Emotional and Physical

In my early years I was very logical; the first book I read was at aged five and was an A-Z encyclopedia approximately 600 Pages long. I could not understand why the story did not make sense, as prior to this I had only experienced story books. I knew my times tables up to and including the twelve tables before I started year one.

Being logical and high achieving academically was positive for me, however, my logic strength sometimes became a weakness. I would often be able to understand flaws in the content and delivery of my parents' arguments and would often highlight these flaws either through smirking, or verbal expression when they were directed at me. This of course would often lead to further punishments, often physical. As a child, the idea that anything could be wrong with how I was treated never occurred to me.

The most common form of abuse I received was verbal. My parents did not understand that it was not okay to constantly yell at a child, for small inconveniences, nor did they understand that blaming a child for perceived slights was also not okay. One example of verbal abuse involved me playing with a toy. I had not played with this toy for a while, and when my mother saw this toy, she asked where I had stolen it from. Confused I answered my toy box, which was not the answer she was looking for. This led to a lot of accusations that I (at six years of age) should know where I stole the toy from and that I was only lying so I could keep it; this led inevitably to physical punishment and the toy being taken off me.

Whilst I cannot remember this incident, it has impacted how I think about property, and impacted my self-image: I have difficulty throwing old stuff away and instead will donate it, I value my "stuff" ahead of other people (excluding my wife and children), I am overly honest in my opinion when asked and am triggered when my honesty is questioned. For me as a parent, I still find it difficult to understand why my mother assumed I stole something, rather than working towards where the toy had come from.

Unknown to me as a child, I was very different socially and had difficulty making friends. During year three at my second primary school, I apparently stole money off my parents for a month. My parents used to keep cash under their bed, and even though I was fed at home, I stole money so that I could buy tuck-shop food at school for myself and peers. Money was very tight for my family, and so when my parents found out, I was severely punished.

Another example of where my mother's reaction was not appropriate was when I received a book from the school Book Club. My parents saved enough money for me to buy a book from the school Book Club and I chose a glow in the dark skeleton information book. I was super excited when I received it as it was exactly what I wanted. However, when I showed my parents the book, my excitement was short lived, as I got into trouble for the book not being worth what they had paid, which somehow became my fault for wanting that book. As punishment for this the book was then taken from me and only given back years later. This specific event has impacted me in a very obvious way with books being my favourite "stuff" to collect and keep and that particular book being on display in the "favourites" section of my library despite it being written for pre-teens.

One example of abuse that did not start out involving my parents, involved an older child introduced into my family home who would often use his size to intimidate and bully me. For just under a year, we had an older child living with us, because his mother was involved in a domestically violent relationship, and my mother knew his mother socially. One incident with the older child involved me washing dishes. I had been asked to wash the dishes, and as most children my age would do, I complained and came up with excuses to get out of it.

The then fifteen-year-old decided that while my mother was in the garage downstairs, he would "encourage" me to wash the dishes. This encouragement involved him standing on my foot with his heel digging in until the top of my foot was broken (the bruise on the top of my foot lasted almost a year). The pain was so much that I screamed, which brought my mother upstairs, much to my relief (albeit short lived relief). Instead of punishing the fifteen-year-old for attacking me, I was then verbally abused, and again this led to physical punishment for screaming and not washing the dishes. I feel that this event has been catalogued in my brain yet another example of where my safety and protection was my own responsibility and may have led to my love of martial arts later in life. To further this point, I was never asked if I was okay and was never taken to a doctor, but I knew I broke my foot as it hurt to walk combined with the bruising lasting so long.

Later in life I would break my foot again but this time in martial arts, and the symptoms of the break were very similar if not the same as the dishes event. As an adult, when I get injured due to my fitness and martial arts pursuits, I will tell my wife. If she responds in a way that I feel is not empathetic, I am triggered beyond what would be considered normal. Once I calm down, and discuss the situation with my wife, I am able to understand that any lack of empathic response by my wife, triggers reexperiencing of my foot event, and the lack of care I received then.

Often when the verbal tactics of my parents were unsuccessful to their intended level, a variety of punishments were given. Minor examples included – being forced to eat a roast meal with a single chopstick because I had been eating too fast at the dinner table, being forced to drink a one litre cup of black unsweetened coffee for making a "bad cup of coffee on purpose", being told that I could attend a party in year eight if I rode the 20kms by bike only to then be picked up half way by my parents and brought back home (as they didn't expect me to actually attempt it), being forced to rewrite my year ten science text book as punishment for skipping one detention at school, being forced to eat a whole grapefruit (as I didn't like sour food) and being forced to eat 1kg of unsweetened plums when I pestered my mother while she was trying to make a plum dessert.

There was also a variety of more regular examples. I was forced almost weekly to stand at the end of the parents' bed at night while they slept for being disrespectful (with more physical punishment if I was caught sleeping or sitting when my mother woke) and had to stay there until my mother allowed me to go to my bed to sleep. To this day I cannot stand still even when important to do so.

If I back-chatted or swore I would have to hold a tablespoon of diced chilli in my mouth until my mother allowed me to swallow it, and if I swallowed any before I was allowed too, I would have to start again with another tablespoon of diced chilli; or if I swore, I would have to brush my teeth with soap and hold it in my mouth until I was allowed to spit.

Another regular punishment involved me having my toys either smashed, cut, or broken in front of me or given to my younger sister as a punishment to me (occasionally within a week of receiving them for my birthday or Christmas). On one occasion my mother tried to smash my toy with a hammer but it kept bouncing off the toy's rubber wings, which made me smile, but determined to break my toy my mother found scissors, cut the wings and then threw the toy into the bin.

One regular occurrence that was not quite a punishment but was still a negative, is how I was taught to catch. When I was younger, my mother would throw jars of coffee at me, often using the 500gram Maxwell coffee jars, with the threat of having to pay for it myself if I dropped them. Again, at the time I did not think it was fair, but also did not see anything wrong with this until later in life when I discussed this with other people.

An emotional experience that was not directly a punishment but had an emotional effect on me was my final experience of owning a pet. The day it died, started like any other, I placed the guinea pigs into the timber and wire box on the grass so they had food, and it was my job to top the water as it was especially hot that day. I did not fill the water bowl enough and my pet died. The day prior to this my guinea pig and my sister's guinea pig had eaten through their cardboard dividers and attacked each other which left a scab across the nose of my guinea pig. When my guinea pig died, my mother made it very clear to me that it was my fault the pet had died, as the guinea pig would have died from being "cooked from the inside out". This was an attempt by my mother to teach me a lesson in responsibility; although at around ten years of age I did not understand why she said this.

A lesser pet example involved my parents' budgerigar. We were cleaning the bird cages in the dining room area while the two budgies flew around. Towards the end of the process my father opened the door to the kitchen and the budgie flew away and never returned. Again, I was blamed for not telling my father the budgie was there and for not stopping it.

A non-pet emotional example involved a friend leaving our town. During year three, my then best friend and friendly competitor left our town. This was the first important friendship that I had lost so I was sad. When I went home and cried about this, I was yelled at. Whilst I didn't receive any form of physical punishment for crying, it did teach me the importance of trying to hide sadness from my family. As an adult, I believe this led to many of anger responses following, and may have further stunted my emotional understanding on top of my Autism (undiagnosed at the time).

Another example of an odd parenting response that was part-punishment part-something-else involved the long drives on holidays, although I cannot remember the holidays. I have, and always have had, light sensitive eyes. Sunglasses were okay for periods, but I could only wear them periodically, as my hypervigilance could see every scratch on the glass. To return to the driving example with my light sensitivity. Whenever we went on long drives, I would often sleep during the day to avoid the light. My parents always packed enough food for everyone, and it was often well organised. Because I slept during the day on the drives, I was often awake at night while my parents drove and of course was hungry.

Instead of allowing me to eat the prepared food, my parents would often punish me for being asleep during the day and allow me to have the minimal amount of food they thought appropriate. This minor example does not seem like much comparatively, however, it did further increase the resentment towards my sister. As this meant that any food I was not allowed at night, she was allowed the next day. Since starting my job as a psychologist I have since found out, that my light sensitivity was yet another sign of my ASD, known as sensory overload.

The last event I feel was negative but would not necessarily be considered abuse involved when I was sick. There were many times as a child that I was sick involving vomit. My parents had a rule that if I were to vomit and did not make it to a sink or a bucket, I must have done so on purpose. As a result, it was my responsibility to clean it, but if I couldn't or did not, I would be punished.

The final type of punishment I often received was physical. I was fortunate that any physical punishment received from my parents, did not leave a bruise, nor break any bones. However, its effects are still felt within me today. Spanking or smacking was one of the main forms of physical punishment which occurred mostly at home, but would also happen in other locations such as the shops, while crossing the road, etc. As well as this, I also received various other physical punishments. My parents had a drawer in a cupboard filled with various belts, and the belt of choice being a plaited brown leather belt with the main target area being my bottom.

Almost daily I received slaps to the face. If I was to flinch or move, I would receive double the number of slaps to the face, and the best coping strategy I developed involved me closing my eyes and taking the hit, (although it took until I was about twelve for me to figure this out). Whilst closing my eyes and taking the hit was successful, I was annoyed it took me so long to figure this out. It felt like once I had worked out that closing my eyes was a viable strategy, the frequency of this punishment slowly decreased. As a result of the face slapping, I am easily triggered whenever anything goes near my face unexpectedly, although this has improved a small amount, since having my own children.

The biggest incident with my father involved me being dragged by the ear, then physically picked up and then thrown down the length of the hallway and crashing into my door. I thought this only happened once and would often joke with my peers that my father taught me to "fly" when I was twelve, however during the process of this book, my sister informed me that this happened more than once. She said that while I was only thrown the length of the hallway once, I would often be dragged by the ear and thrown small distances by our father for not listening. I have also learnt that sharing this type of punishment as a flight joke often made other people feel uncomfortable and have worked hard to discontinue the joke.

A section like this can often be very emotional and can lead the listener or reader to ask many other questions. I will add here that I was not a victim of any sexual assault; and all the discussed abuse and trauma stemmed from a misguided ideology that pain is the best tool to teach discipline and life's lessons such as resilience and respect. Whilst I do not like the cyclic argument as an excuse for poor behavioural choices, I understand that my parents' childhoods and upbringing, did not teach them any positive parenting tools. My parents also had a fridge magnet that said, "do as I say, not as I do", which they strongly followed in their parenting ethos.

I feel that as a child I thought fear meant respect in the context of a parent child relationship. This idea that fear meant respect still impacts my parenting ability today. When my new parenting skills that I continuously have to work on, do not work, I revert back to a fear/control response where I will use an angry face to instil fear in my own children. It is something that I am not proud of, and as stated, I try daily to not to use it.

I feel the use of the heading "silent abuse" was fitting in explaining my experience. For most of my life no one knew or wanted to know about my experiences, and it was not until I spoke more with my friend James that I felt I could share some of my experiences. In 2013 I started volunteering for a mental health organisation and was once again able to start talking about my experiences, and this time use my negatives as a positive tool in discussion with young people.

Low Income Family and our Neighbours

When I was still an infant, my parents lived with my aunty Ruth for a short period. Ruth had a child thirteen days younger than myself and money was very tight. One example my mother has shared over time involved a fight between her and Ruth and "the old cow" (Ruth's and my mother's mother). My mother and Ruth were arguing over a last item of food, so my mother tried to stab Ruth with a double ended pencil, and unfortunately stabbed herself in the hand, if this wasn't bad enough "the old cow" hit my mother across the head with a frying pan. I feel this example sets the scene about our finance and childhoods.

My family was fortunate enough to have a stable location to live and not have to worry about government housing or rental properties. There were some occasions where my mother would go without food to ensure my sister and I had enough food for school, and other occasions where we would line up to receive a government hamper for $10 which included a box of various foods.

My sister and I were fortunate enough to have some pocket money in our earliest years, and when our parents needed to borrow some of our pocket money, they would write how much they owed us. To help our parents' financial situation, we would often lessen the amount they owed us, without their knowledge. Later when my father lost his job, we were given whatever five cent pieces our parents had available. With the five cent pieces I was once able to save twenty dollars.

One pertinent event that demonstrated our financial situation involved a twenty-cent coin. My mother had dropped a twenty-cent coin on her way into the kitchen. My sister, my mother, and I then spent approximately twenty minutes looking for this coin in the garden it fell into. We eventually found it on the corner of the step.

Another event that I believe demonstrated our financial situation involves collecting cans. My mother, my sister and I would walk the streets in our town collecting cans and bottles and place them into garbage bags. We would then take the bags to the local aluminium metal place, have the bags, and weighed and be paid per kilogram.

We had several neighbours in close proximity, and there were several children in our street around my age, some of which I went to school with. The one house in our street that had air-conditioning was known as the "rich neighbours" and was where I had two of my first paying jobs.

There was a time of about a year when my aunty Ruth and her three children lived next door to us. I considered this a positive, as it allowed me twelve months of emotional escape, as I was my aunt's favourite because she had three daughters and always wanted a son. Thankfully, I did not understand the many difficulties my cousins experienced living with their mother Ruth, so I had only positive memories and emotions about her until I was an adult.

There was also a time of about two years when my maternal grandfather Dale lived next door to us. We were often reminded by Dale, that he was a "Sergeant Major" in the British military "back in the days when you could carry a hitting stick". During the two-year period he lived next door, he would often walk us to the bus stop at the end of the street. He would walk his own pace and if we wanted to "keep up" we had to either learn to walk fast or run. The one sports event he attended of mine involved me competing in triple jump at a school athletics day. It was a cold day with strong cold wind, so I chose to wear my jacket to compete. This led Dale to start being verbally aggressive about me wearing a jacket and that I was not serious about the competition. He then made it quite clear how to perform the exercise correctly, often discussing everything I was doing wrong, drawing again from his military days where he was the triple jump champion in his battalion.

I am told he loved us, however, his inability to express this to a child, his opinion about how to treat children, and his over critical verbal comments, overrode any love he may have shown. I attended his funeral after he died from stomach cancer, but refused to look at his deceased body in the coffin. During the funeral, I unexpectedly cried. Perhaps I cried because it had some unknown emotional connection to him, but I felt the main reason I cried was because of how fantastic everyone kept saying he was. He reportedly had assisted at a hospital, had published several books about medicine that included illustrations, and even had his own memoir typed up by my mother (however, his memoir only focused on his Caucasian son, and did not mention his three older half Indian daughters or any of his illegitimate children). Following his funeral, I developed a saying that "you cannot be a great person and a good person", meaning that you can be a good father, spend time with your kids, not beat your family etc., or you can be like my grandfather and be a horrible person at home, but do great things for the community.

Looking back as an adult, I believe he may have had some positive emotion towards us, such as love, as he painted our sheds with his artwork. When he and his third wife lived next door, they would also occasionally invite us over for afternoon tea, at his wife's request. With one positive event being his Japanese wife's jelly that was made from seaweed but tasted as good as the sweet shop version.

Strength in Academic Pursuit and Sporting Achievements

One way I was able to function and enjoy life when I was younger was through my thirst for knowledge and competition. School was a welcome escape from home and despite my home environment and the constant school bullying I was able to perform well academically. I was often in the top two in any of my classes at school, with my biggest academic downfall being my messy writing, which led me to make a myriad of mistakes because of the confusion that stemmed from not being able to read my own writing. I recently discovered a folder full of various academic awards from math, German, and science supporting my claim of early academic success. The highlight of my early years academically was the two inter-school competitions. The first trip was a regional academic inter-school competition and following our team's success; we then went to the state-wide competition. Whilst our school did not do that well at state level, it was still a great experience.

I enjoyed attending school, possibly as an escape from home, possibly because of my thirst for knowledge; however, I learnt at a young age that class politics, and who you know, impacts most things. At the end of year six, I applied for school captain. After the voting was completed, it was announced that I had been chosen as school vice-captain. However, the teachers at the small-town school were not happy with this as their children did not hold any leadership positions, so a "recount" was held. Following this "recount" all the teacher's children and children who had particular last names, held leadership positions and I did not. Following this I never again went for a leadership position in that primary school or following high schools. I felt if politics can impact events that involved kids, there was no point in trying. This is probably one area that does not fit well with my need for competition, but I still feel today that politics does impact various aspects of life. However, I also understand there are still many areas that I can control and instead put my effort into that, and hope my social networking and my skill level are enough to counter any of these negative social politics.

Outside of school my parents tried to get me engaged in social activities such as sport. I was involved in rugby league at age six and was awarded an age champion medal; was involved in 'Little Athletics' and again was awarded an aged champion medal. Later, I would later find karate and other martial arts where I was very successful at various competitions.

<u>Early signs of an ASD brain</u>

One social event my sister and I attended for many of my childhood years, was 'Sunday School'. The local church held a children's social event weekly involving arts and craft, food, and religious stuff. My family was not religious, but it was one of the only social events that was held in my town and was free to attend. Eventually, we stopped attending the church's social activities with one possible reason involving my confusion of the content they were teaching.

After one of the craft events and discussion around the church's belief system, I came home and asked why god was my father and why the man whom I had been calling dad was not my father. My logical brain was confused as the church had used the term "father" and I interpreted this as meaning biological father. This angered my Atheist mother and led to various punishments towards myself, and an angry conversation between my mother and the local church. A key positive feeling I have, regarding the church in my town involved the church's garage sales. They held regular garage sales and one weekend they sold an old Sega console for five dollars, which I still have today. My sister reminded me that I also used to enjoy attending the social event as they would often have nice cake.

Another event that I feel may be related to ASD misinterpretation of social situations involves when I had a friend visiting. I was between twelve and thirteen and invited my friend to listen to some music. At the time I was enjoying a CD with the hits of the eighties. One of the songs was Macarena and I started playing this. My mother then came into the room and told me to turn it off. After my friend left, she told me that I should play that type of music while friends were over as they might think that I was gay. Looking back, I am still unsure if this was my poor social awareness, in not being able to know what was appropriate or not in social situations, or if it was mother having different ideas about what boys were allowed to do in public.

Ignorance and Sarcasm

I believe the saying "ignorance is bliss" was pertinent in my situation growing up. Since communication with neighbour's kids never focused on our home lives, I perceived the type of punishments I received as normal. I felt that I had no perceived reason to be unhappy as I was fed, had school, and had a place to live. It was not until I met my friends later in life that I began to understand that most of my experiences were not normal and therefore not okay. Mental health topics such as mental illness, suicide or self-harm were also taboo in my town back then, so if I ever did have any thoughts of ending my life (and was able to remember them), I probably would not have had the language to express it anyway. The only conversations we ever had about mental illness involved one of my mother's sisters who was known as the "crazy one". I use this concept today to explain to some young people, that when I grew up you were either in a straitjacket like my aunty, or you ate metaphorical concrete. This obviously was not helpful but was the norm.

Sarcasm was the main tool I used as a child, at home and school often without thinking before speaking. This meant I was a bit of class clown at times towards fellow students and teachers. On one occasion I pushed the sarcasm too far with a peer in year eight and was punched in the face. Another example of my sarcasm and fear of my parents involves my grade eight music class. I was being a class clown and my teacher gave me two opportunities to listen. After ignoring the teacher for a third time, he gave me a detention slip, which led to me crying in front of the class. After class, he had a conversation with me and asked why I was crying. To which I explained that I did not care about the detention, but if my parents received notice that I had one more detention at school, I would receive a lot of punishment when I returned home. Of course, by year eight, my mother still had a certain reputation, so the teacher removed the detention slip and from then on would use the threat of detention to ensure I listened in class.

For me sarcasm and humour combined, made the most difficult situations more bearable and made it easier to manage negative emotions. Despite the occasional negative implications of using sarcasm, it was a tool I continued to use as the perceived benefits outweighed the perceived negatives. It is also a tool I continue to use as an adult to manage daily stressors, social gatherings and occasionally during professional work meetings.

Another unspoken positive of using sarcasm is occasionally I am wrong about a topic, but people assume I am being sarcastic, so in their eye I am still right. This idea further encourages my use of sarcasm, and I am getting better at knowing when not to use it when speaking with professional colleagues. I am also aware that there is a chance that my sarcasm may be heard as passive-aggressive communication, and that I should choose when to be sarcastic.

First Signs of Mental Illness, Misdiagnosed, and then Ignored by Parents

The first time I received a mental illness diagnosis was when I was around seven years of age. Following several years of my high energy and poorly managed anger, I was diagnosed by the General Practitioner with Attention Deficit Hyperactivity Disorder (ADHD). My parents ignored this diagnosis as they believed that ADHD was over diagnosed, and that mental illnesses were only for crazy people (such as my Aunty, who spent time in a straitjacket). It was not until I found karate in high school, and my anger improved, that one of my parents took credit for ignoring the ADHD diagnosis. As an adult I would eventually be diagnosed with Asperger Syndrome and Post Traumatic Stress Disorder.

My continuing aggressive behaviour at home and school were possible signs of trauma, although back then in my hometown, mental health knowledge was not very advanced, and rarely spoken about. Teachers were also ill-equipped to understand mental illness in my town where I grew up, but thankfully, I had several teachers that still tried to support me.

The main event that I believe demonstrated clear signs of ASD when I was a child, was when our family pet 'Lassie' died. He was a German Shepard cross with a Collie and, was with our family for about ten years. Unfortunately, Lassie died when he was bitten by several Redback spiders during the night. The day he died my father was crying and I attempted to do the correct thing by trying to console him. My logical brain understood our financial situation, and the amount of money it cost to feed Lassie; so, trying to be helpful, I said "at least we will save money on pet food". This of course led to severe physical punishments, and my parents did not bother questioning why I said that statement.

During my primary school years, my high functioning ASD was also prevalent and supported by my teachers. I was often provided textbooks and other resources of content from more senior grades. I feel that this extra effort and support from my primary school teachers assisted in my love for school and learning.

<u>Unknown Support Person</u>

It was not until I was nineteen that I would realise that throughout my childhood I had a constant and often unappreciated ally in my younger sister. My younger sister comparatively had an easy childhood; however, she also received her share of cruel and unusual punishments and experienced her own trauma. Whilst it may be helpful to discuss some of her stories, I have chosen to limit the amount of information I share about my sister and of her negative experiences, as she is not comfortable sharing these due to her own ongoing mental health struggles.

Growing up my sister would often be shielded by a lot of the abuse by our father, and this combined with punishments such as my toys being given to her, led to an unacknowledged resentment towards her.

My sister has since told me that she often would stand up for me when I was bullied at school, and occasionally question a parenting decision even when it was not in her best interest. She has often told me that she wishes she had my ability to block out our childhood memories as she often struggles with the flashbacks of our respective childhoods, leading to her own mental health concerns. Even though I would not know or appreciate my sister's efforts until I was nineteen, I am glad I had her support. I feel that my inability to visualise and see images while conscious has allowed me to improve my mental health, with much more ease than my sister.

James and My Loss of Memory Pre-Twelve

In year eight at my local high school, I made a small group of friends with whom I still talk to. One of the friends in the group was James. James was in the same social group as myself in year eight and most of year nine, before I moved to North Queensland. After knowing James, a year or so, I was invited to his house a couple of times including an overnight stay. I learnt a lot from that sleep over that I would not appreciate until many years later. The first lessons I learnt from spending time with James' family was that married people don't have to argue and yell at each other every night before bed, and that married people could actually love each other and not just stay together for the sake of the children. My parents would often make snide remarks about couples who did not argue, and this combined with their daily arguments, led me to believe that married people did not like each other.

The overnight stay at James's house, would eventually help shape how I parent, and showed me a glimpse of what a healthy marriage looked like. None of this wisdom was understood or appreciated at the time, however. James would also be called upon later when my mental health started to decline, when I needed relationship advice, a different perspective, or needed a distraction from suicidal thoughts.

Many years later, I was having a conversation with my best mate James and I was telling him how it is sometimes annoying that I cannot remember before I was twelve years of age. This conversation took place around the middle of 2017, and it was not until this conversation that I realised my interpersonal memory had not always been so bad. James told me that in year eight I would often tell him some of the stuff that happened to me at home and we would sometimes discuss this (as best twelve to thirteen-year-old children can). He even remembered me telling him about my mornings before school. Almost every morning of year eight and nine at my country town high school, I would walk to high school crying each morning (because of home events) but would ensure the tears were wiped away before I arrived at the school grounds.

Due to my loss of memory, the earliest childhood memory I have is when I was twelve years of age. The main positive of not remembering before I was twelve, is that I am unable to consciously remember any childhood events, although the impact is still felt today. The biggest negative of losing my memory of before I was twelve is, when people reference experiences, cartoons, pop culture, or reminisce, I am unable to relate, and this can bring unwanted sadness in an otherwise happy context.

I also cannot remember the positive experiences from when I was young, including any holidays we had as a family or any positive experiences I had with the neighbour's children. This is most evident when spending time with my wife's family. They often discuss their positive or silly memories of when they were young, and all I have to share is negative memories of abuse, etc. Another difficulty I have relating to others' stories is my early achievement, despite no memory of it compared to many people's childhoods. This becomes more difficult at my wife's family gatherings as most of their stories focus on being academically average which I struggle relating to.

Again, my wife's family often share stories of their silly behaviours when they were young, but all I have to share are my various sporting and academic achievements and awards, which can often lead to awkward conversation. Occasionally at my wife's family gatherings I will try to share a personal story, so as to be part of the conversation but mine are often much more negative which only leads to more awkwardness.

There are two main theories that I feel explain why I cannot remember my childhood. The first is related to PTSD and the second related to ASD. The PTSD theory suggests my brain has a "brain block" that serves as a protective factor regarding my childhood and that whilst I have the ability to solve complex visual puzzles in real life scenarios, I am unable to see the processing (like a black box). The second theory suggests that my ASD interpretation of my childhood has less focus on interpersonal relationships and more focus on facts and theories.

12-15-year-old
First Paid jobs

Hard work was and still is, one of my core values, and I often tell people how I had my first paying job at age twelve. When I was twelve, I had wants like most other kids, and the most expensive of all was the 'Star Wars' weekly information sheets that came in the Sunday edition of the newspaper. Having minimal money, and because of my age; I asked neighbours for work.

I was offered work with one neighbour as a potato picker. This was before machinery did it, and it involved digging potatoes with your hands and filling hessian sacks capable of carrying twenty kilograms each. As a potato picker you were paid per sack; however, as I was only twelve my neighbours offered me twelve dollars for twelve hours work, which I was more than happy with. This was apparently a form of child exploitation, but as a twelve-year-old with no money I was unaware of any wrongdoing by the neighbours.

Later our "wealthy neighbour" offered me a mowing job, where I had to use a push mower to mow her yard, her dogs play yard, and then wash the mower. For this job I earnt twenty dollars, which was enough to buy a copy of the 'Star Wars' information every second week unless it rained. The other odd paid jobs I worked at ages twelve to thirteen involved waiting tables at the high school social event (this is where I got my first tip of fifty cents) and waiting at our wealthy neighbour's fondue social events.

High School Achievements and Supportive People

During my one year and three terms at my country town high school, I earned various academic and sporting achievements. My academic achievements while at the local high school included – being in a subject known as "advanced study" which involved science, chess, mathematics, and language and was only offered to a select few; competing in local mathematics competitions and representing the high school at a German language competition where I came second.

Early in year eight at the local high school I discovered Karate. One of the school's science teachers Mat was also a qualified Karate instructor and held lunchtime training sessions in the school's drama room. This was the first big positive event I remember, as martial arts gave me an outlet for most of my anger, gave me social connection, and gave me the competition that I seemed to enjoy. Mat and his family also assisted with the training fees when my parents could not afford them, assisted in providing me with a training Gi and would eventually offer me free training at the main Karate dojo in south Brisbane. On several occasions I was also given the chance to train at another karate dojo in Brisbane which belonged to Mat's sensei, which was a rare honour for myself.

When I would return to Brisbane for university, his family allowed me to live with them almost rent free (fifty dollars a fortnight including food, electricity, and lodging). I also learnt valuable life skills about family, how siblings could have occasional arguments but still love each other and that being different within the family context was also okay. The lessons I learnt from their family combined with what I learnt from my friend James' family led to me having a positive framework for when I had my own family.

As well as Mat, there was another teacher at the school involved with the Karate who helped me more than she needed to. My German subject teacher Margaret and her extended family assisted with my karate training through giving me opportunities to train outside of school hours. When possible, she would drive me to the training in south Brisbane (approximately a forty-five-minute drive); buy me take away for dinner after training, and occasionally stop by her mother's house so her mother could give me the left-over bread from the bakery she worked at, to take home for my family. Sometimes I would return home with multiple black garbage bags full of bread, that we were able to freeze.

I would go on to win various karate events in solo Kumite, solo Kata and team Kata, and participate in various Karate demonstrations in and around the Brisbane district before being forced to move to North Queensland.

Change of Towns

Towards the end of year nine we had to sell our house for financial reasons as my father severely injured his back at his previous work, due to unsafe work practices by his employer. He did find other work and still had several months left at his new job when my parents chose to move. We moved to North Queensland (NQ) where my aunty Ruth was living, because my father still had to finish work, I was given a choice: stay in the local town (living in an old caravan with my father in the backyard of our neighbour's residence), or move to North Queensland and live in a house (but have to start a new school).

Being very logical, I chose the caravan option purely because of a Karate grading I had coming up. Despite being offered a choice, and despite choosing to stay in my current school, I was forced to move to North Queensland with my mother and sister. Many years later, I was told that my mother reportedly believed I chose my father "over her" when I said I wanted the caravan option. The public high school I left had a total of three hundred and sixty children, and the public high school I attended in North Queensland had over one thousand and four hundred children.

This was a huge change of culture for me, but I was fortunate as I was able to be involved with my cousin's social group for the final term of year nine. Whilst it was obvious that I "did not fit in" with my cousin's friends, it made the transition from a small-town high school to a large high school a lot easier. The culture change was huge for various reasons. Firstly, the size of the school both in student numbers and in building size was massive compared to what I had grown up with, and secondly, the difference in school culture from the administrative team through to the student level.

During the enrolment process the administration made it very clear to me (in person) that they believed my A grades that I had earnt in a country high school were only worth a C in their school (class politics, once again shaping my perception). This taught me that I did not have to work hard academically because class politics affected the outcome anyway, so there was no reason to try. By the time, the school realised their error and placed me back in the classes I should have been enrolled in, I had lost interest in trying academically, and instead turned to school sport.

My best sporting achievements at the school involved the running event known as cross country and athletics, with my main event being triple jump. In cross country I came fifth at the school level and twentieth in the North Queensland region, and in athletics I finished fourth in North Queensland. With the top three positions moving onto the state competition. Regarding my placing in triple jump, I felt that once again politics may have played a part. The person who was measuring the jumps came from the same school as the student who reportedly beat me by one centimetre. This event on its own may not have impacted me, however due to my many life experiences prior to this, where politics had taken away opportunities, I felt that once again, I had been unfairly treated. This did however, highlight the importance of networking, although I didn't realise this lesson until many years later.

The second big culture change was the social culture from the peer level up. Due to the large population at the high school, there were many more social groups than I was used to (although they did still have the stereotypical groups such as your sporting group, geek and nerd groups) and the sheer size of the school was intimidating. When I arrived at the large high school, I had a hair style affectionately known as a 'Mullet', which made me stand out of the crowd. When I first started at the city high school, I used to use gel in my hair, thinking that I had to look respectable at a city school compared to a country town high school. However, I quickly observed that no one used gel and that a messy mullet was more socially acceptable.

Thankfully for me my mullet haircut worked in my social favour, and I was quickly known and able to spend time in many of the lunch time groups and make many superficial social connections. The 'mullet' also hid or satirised my otherwise social awkwardness as I did not fit neatly into any of the social groups at the massive high school. The many social nuances I had to learn the hard way may have been signs of my ASD. When I eventually chose to cut my hair, my superficial popularity declined, but I was still able to sit with and socialise with two different social groups (the "nerds" and the "sports" groups).

During my time at the high school, I was only involved in two physical fights that lasted several minutes. These fights were fair, one on one and had no long-term implications. Despite being fifteen, many of my peers consumed alcohol, and various other substances, which I was not interested in trying. This meant that I was invited to less parties as a result and those I was invited to attend, I did not stay for long because I was bored being one of the only sober people there. There were various times where I was teased, based on misunderstandings, or my refusal to change, but the main negative teasing I received was based on my taste in music. During an English class I admitted I enjoyed rap music, which led to various insults. The teasing itself did not impact me greatly but highlighted how important the music was to me. As an adult looking back, it is obvious I used music a lot to help get me through difficult emotions, with heavy rock and rap music being the main genres.

As a side note regarding moving from the small town to North Queensland, there was an event that impacted me that had nothing to do with abuse or being bullied. The month leading up to our move I was allowed to take photos with all the people I felt had been positive for me during my time at the small-town high school. There were a small group of people three years senior to me whom had always been nice to me and I wanted to remember them as well as several people in my friends' group and several other peers my age. Several month later after my family had settled in with my aunty, we had the film printed. Unfortunately, the photo printing shop tried their best to print the photos but told us that the film was blank and possibly faulty. I felt very sad and cried a lot. This was in a time when I did not know what social media was, and I knew we couldn't afford to return to Brisbane for a long time. Thankfully, many years later, I would slowly be in contact with some of the people and find the others on social media.

As will be mentioned again later, one thing that helped me get through difficult experiences was music. When I was allowed to go to bed and didn't have to stand at the end of my parents' bed, music helped drown out the parents' arguing and my own thoughts.

15-19

<u>Parent's Divorce and Parental Engagement</u>
For some children when their parents' divorce, it brings about a large amount of negative emotion and negative challenges. However, for me I did not feel much negative emotion about the separation, as I chose to focus on what the news would mean for me. I made the decision to stay with the parent who fulfilled my geographical or personal needs the most.

One of my parents had been working away a lot, and a mutual friend of my parents moved in with us. After a long period of time, with one parent working away, my parents separated. They separated after a questionable relationship one of them had with the family friend that was living with us. My father chose to move west, while my mother chose to stay where we were in North Queensland. I was given the choice of moving west or staying, and I chose to stay so I could complete high school. My sister chose to go west with the parent that had protected her from most of the abuse; and possibly to escape our mother.

Following the divorce, my father slowly stopped engaging with me and began being more selfish. I did visit him out west on several occasions, but invitations to visit slowly stopped. My father would eventually stop talking to me until approximately two and a half years later, including no birthday card or letter for my 18th. Eventually my sister returned to live with our mother again.

Following this our father would visit, officially to say hello to both my sister and I. However, many years later, my sister told me that he would often bring her gifts such as chocolates but would never bring me one. To protect my feelings, my sister and mother chose to not tell me. My father eventually met a colleague at his new job and married. Once married my father inherited two stepchildren, which meant he had even less time for myself and for my sister.

My mother continued the abuse towards me, but this slowly decreased. It may have been because I was becoming the same size as her. However, I feel the more realistic reason was because I had finally figured out that if I closed my eyes and took a hit (to the face or other), and did not respond with emotion, the punishment was over sooner. On the surface, it also appeared that her new relationship with the family friend was less stressful, as they did not argue every night prior to going to sleep. Another possible reason she slowed and then stopped the abuse was because she was also a victim of emotional abuse (not that I knew this at the time) but regardless of what the cause was, the lack of abuse was welcome.

My parents have told my sister and I that they stayed together for so many years for us as they did not want us to live in a broken home. However, I strongly believe that they would have been better off emotionally, if they had separated many years prior, and perhaps my sister and I would have received less abuse. It is evident that neither of my parents enjoy being alone for long, and both parents have often moved from partner to partner with minimal time in-between.

For reasons unknown to me, when I was between nineteen and twenty, my father began to reengage, with a period where he often would remember my birthday, possibly with help from his new wife. I met my wife when I was nineteen, and she did not meet him personally until several years into our relationship.

Since having my children my father has continued some engagement but has forgotten about my birthdays on a consistent basis and even his engagement with my children has begun to decline including forgetting about their birthdays.

First Love

Like most people my first love was a high school relationship. I was a sexually naïve teenage male, who had zero experience in romantic relationships, and had never kissed a girl. When I was approximately fifteen, I decided to cut my 'mullet', but I did not expect the social change that would happen.

I lost my group of younger friends who would follow me everywhere, and I slowly lost my superficial social status among my peers, but I slowly started to put some of my own identity together. Best of all, I began my first romantic relationship. My girlfriend Tara taught me a lot about relationships, and a lot about sexual education. Her parents were somewhat nice to my face but felt that as I was from a broken home, and I was not religious that I may corrupt their "good Christian girl".

Of course, the opposite was true, and their daughter taught me a lot about sex that she had learnt from her first experience from her partner a year or more before she met me. Tara's mother also told us early into the relationship, that I should not get too attached, as the relationship probably would not work out anyway as "first relationships never did". Whilst

Tara's mother became correct several months later, it seemed an odd thing to say to a fifteen-year-old.

Tara's social contacts also helped me start my first official job at a local IGA as a delicatessen team member; after school, and on the weekends. Whilst the relationship with Tara would eventually end after eleven months as I was "too boring", I learned a lot, including some basic social and hygiene skills such as communicating with groups of people, and cleaning under toe nails. Both may seem obvious, but due to my ASD brain, I had to be taught. Also, as Tara was in a large friend group, dating Tara allowed me to make some good friendships within that friend group. Some of those friendships lasted for twelve years, and some of the people in the friend group, such as Greta, I continue to communicate with to this day.

From North Queensland to Brisbane and Back

When my family moved to North Queensland, and we had our own rental, I was eventually allowed to start martial arts again. The only one my parents could afford and knew a small amount about was a Tae Kwon Do dojo nearby that taught Rhee Tae Kwon Do. I was allowed to train here for six months where I graded five belts in two gradings, and started to enjoy the new martial art. However, after six months of training I was forced to stop. I have told many people that I stopped training because the gradings were too easy, and I was bored. However, the real reason I stopped training in Rhee Tae Kwon Do was because my parents thought it was a suitable punishment for a negative behaviour choice I had made. Which made no sense to me, but there was nothing I could do, so I made up a story as to why I stopped. Although many years later, when I asked my parents about why I had to stop training they denied it was a punishment and told me it was for financial reasons.

In year twelve I went for 'sports age champion'. At the school I was attending they did half of the events the week prior and the other half of the events on the big day. Because of my performance in the events prior to the big sports day I was sitting in second place overall, so my goal was looking achievable. However, the very first event of the sports day I twisted my knee while throwing a javelin, then tried to "run it off" by competing in the eight hundred metre event. Following this poor decision to "run it off", I was unable to walk and could not compete in any events on the day. As a result, I ended with an overall ranking of fourth, which was very disappointing to me. Coming fourth meant no recognition of effort via a medal, and all I have to show as evidence of my effort is a cool story.

After graduating from high school in North Queensland with an OP of thirteen (where OP one was the best and twenty-five the worst), I moved back to Brisbane where I lived with Mat and his family for one and a half years. The official and conscious reason I left North Queensland was that the University of Queensland allegedly had a better 'Bachelor of Education' program. In hindsight it was probably an easy way to escape living at home. I was also able to strengthen my friendship with James, strengthen previous high school friendships and finally began to find my own identity as a person who thirsted for knowledge and needed almost constant mental stimulation, but also required the physical competition of sport or martial arts.

While back in Brisbane I returned to the Karate I had trained in previously and quickly graded to Shodan Ho. I competed in various tournaments at the local and city levels winning multiple individual and team events; and was named tournament champion at one of the local tournaments. Unfortunately, I was unable to attend what was supposed to be my final tournament in Brisbane, due to contracting chicken pox and being bed ridden.

I also dabbled in funk and hip-hop dance for a period of six months as James wanted someone he knew, to try it with. In that six-month period, we did several mini concerts at schools, south Brisbane halls and at the Gold Coast. I approached the dancing as I had approached my martial arts; each dance sequence was like my martial arts katas, specific forms or movements in a given sequence. This approach allowed me to learn the needed moves quickly and allowed me mistake free presentations.

During my time attending university in south Brisbane, I made several friends, with whom I still keep in contact with via social media, and I began to focus on social sport, karate, and work instead of studying. I slowly put less and less effort into study and eventually became disinterested in my university study, and instead focused on earning money working. I worked in various jobs such as a meat works, a fast-food restaurant (KFC) and a call centre.

While in Brisbane I met some friends from my KFC job who lived in a town in south Brisbane known as Ipswich. After knowing them for twelve months, one of the KFC managers and friends invited me to a party. The party was held at a two-storey house, and most of the people drinking went upstairs, whereas I stayed downstairs playing pool. I was playing pool with two of my female friends when we heard an aggressive screeching of tires coming from outside. We joked that it was people coming to "gate crash" the party.

Unfortunately, this was accurate and within a couple of minutes six male adults entered the downstairs area. They were evidently high on illicit drugs and were demanding that we tell them where a person named John was. My two friends and I had no idea who they were talking about. After several threats from the gate crashers, the leader threw a pool ball at me and left. This event taught me the importance of positive handling of the event. The whole time they were yelling and screaming, I stood in front of my two female friends and calmly told the gate crashers, that I did not know who they were talking about. We eventually left the party with no more than a bruise on my stomach. We later heard that the gate crashers returned and demolished the house, so I am grateful I was able to be assertive and request to leave when I did.

I eventually decided to apply for the military. I did well in the military's intelligence screening and had all but a couple of flying options available for me to apply. However, I decided just in time, to withdraw my application, following the Brisbane recruiter saying they needed infantry positions and because of my age they would probably stream me towards infantry. After discussions with James and his older sister, it became evident that the military option may have been a way to escape and find purpose; and once I took the time to assess the military option, I was no longer convinced it was the right decision. I am glad I did not complete the military application process, as I have diagnosed PTSD without any military time, so I feel that if I had of joined, my symptoms may have become worse.

During this time in Brisbane, I also had my first alcoholic beverage of Midori and lemonade. I believe the only reason I agreed to this was because James's older sister (who I was attracted to at the time) encouraged me to try it. I only managed to drink half a glass, as I did not want to risk losing any control. One of my coping strategies throughout life (following various negative choices pre-12) has always been to find some way of maintaining control of myself. I believed that if I was to consume too much alcohol this control would be lost, and I would say or do something that I would regret later. While in Brisbane I also had my first stubby of 'Canadian Club' (again only half) at my going away party. I would later try alcohol two more times; once at my 'Bucks night' where I had half a glass of bourbon and coke, and then again at my wedding where I had a sip of champagne.

These are the only four times I have ever consumed alcohol. At times it has been difficult, because it meant I was not invited to social gatherings, because alcohol was often the only way for some of my peers to have fun; but I am often glad to tell people about the limited amount of alcohol I have consumed in my life.

Second Love

My second love happened when I was at university in Brisbane. My female friends had begun creating social media accounts for me such as 'Myspace', 'Bebo' and eventually 'Facebook'. As I was learning how to use 'Myspace' I came across a photo with a friend and her other friends. I enquired about the name of a particular friend and after the mutual friend introduced me, I eventually asked Casey out on a date.

Dating Casey was a positive experience for me for many reasons. I learned a whole lot more about relationships and how relationships worked, my understanding of interpersonal boundaries improved, and I learnt the difference between love, and staying with someone because they were nice to you. Prior to Casey I thought that a positive romantic relationship was where two people never argued and were always nice to each other, as in the opposite to my parents.

Casey had many positive attributes including her caring nature, her intelligence, and her family. However, her inability to express the things she wanted for herself, created an imbalance in the relationship where we did whatever I wanted to do, whenever I wanted to do it. After many conversations with my friend James, I eventually made the tough decision to end the relationship after sixteen months. I tried to break up with Casey in the nicest way possible by taking her on one last date but have since found out that all this may have done is make the separation more difficult for Casey.

It was probably the first time I cared greatly about the decision I was making as I knew it would affect Casey negatively. Casey being hurt was further supported by her attempting to contact me multiple times, me blocking her on social media and her attempting to contact my mother to see how I was. To this day I hope that Casey's life has turned out as fantastic as my life is today.

I will note here, that if it was not for dating Casey, I may never have continued my self-discovery and may not be as good a husband and father as I try to be today.

After ending the relationship with Casey, I eventually moved back to North Queensland and lived with my mother and her partner. While living there I would gradually increase my martial arts training to eighteen hours a week, while maintaining various jobs including – supermarket delicatessen manager, fast food restaurant employee, butcher, bartender, and various others.

Signs of My Mental Illness

The first time I remember being aware that there may be something wrong with my mental health was the first time I had a suicidal thought. I was using the computer in the downstairs garage when the thought of ending my own life felt like a good idea. I remember the knee pain (that had been misdiagnosed as "inflammation" by various bulk billing doctors) was quite intense that day, which then triggered some childhood traumas. The next thought I had was to "play chicken with the cars" that drove past my house on a regular basis. I thought I would try to call James and see if he was able to distract me enough before I went outside. Thankfully for me he answered and was able to chat about stuff I have no memory of, and this was enough to distract me and calm me down. Whilst the thought of ending my life would arise occasionally following this, there was never any intent to die, as I knew I could talk if needed.

I should mention that for as long as I could remember I would have multiple nightmares every night and have trouble getting to sleep every night. The nightmares consisted of me punching and kicking my parents and sister, where I was my actual size and not my childhood size. In my nightmares, I was able to stand up to my parents and get revenge in the situations that I could not and would not do in real life. While having nightmares I would also punch and kick the wall in real life, often leaving indents on the wall.

I often had difficulty sleeping each night because I had too many thoughts, each night and my parents would often be arguing loudly about their relationship, our life and occasionally about me. To counter the noise and to help drown out my thoughts, I would often use the radio to help me sleep. The use of the radio lessened over the years, but the nightmares would continue until I met my final love whom I am now married too. I was unaware that this was not normal, and to the best of my knowledge never discussed this with James at the time.

In the same year I had the suicidal thought, and subsequent phone conversation with James, I also had what I consider to be a breakdown. The morning of my breakdown I had a nightmare the night before that included my father's dead body in graphic detail (even though he is alive). I then rode to work where my boss was once again late and the stress that had previously put on me to complete my role as the delicatessen manager was triggered. I then quit my job, rode home, and locked myself in my room and played rap music on the CD player as loud as I could, in an attempt to get rid of the thought and memory of the graphic nightmare.

My mother's partner at the time, then knocked on the door and told me to turn the music down, and after this request I started crying and shaking uncontrollably. I then told my sister and mother (who happened to be in the hallway by this stage) that for as long as I could remember, I had nightmares where I was able to retaliate; and punch and kick my parents and attack my sister. Just the ability to talk and express my daily nightmares decreased the frequency and severity of them from multiple a night to approximately one a night.

Two other examples regarding my mental illness involved my martial arts training. With some of my training I had a reputation of being hardworking, and having mongrel, as I was able to punch the pads at training until my knuckles bled, and then keep going, until the time was finished. This was often celebrated by some of my martial arts peers. To condition my knuckles, I would often 'roll punch' brick walls or metal poles. I would often do this conditioning of my knuckles when I became bored at social gatherings. At the time of my training and "conditioning", and because of the social environment I was in, I thought this behaviour to be normal because considerable focus in martial arts is placed on conditioning the body.

However, looking back using my unique perspective as a former martial artist and current mental health practitioner, I understand that punching brick walls, and metal poles is not conditioning but actually a form of self-harm. This self-harm may have been used at the time to channel any annoyance I had in a way that was accepted by my peers. The punching of poles and walls continued sporadically until the birth of my first son, where I no longer felt the need to "condition my knuckles".

During my time training in martial arts an event happened that reinforced the need to train. My mother's partner at the time had an older brother who had a fling with my married aunty. When this ended and my mother said something to the brother, he threatened to burn our house down. Because of the family he was from the threat felt like a real possibility rather than an empty threat. Upon being told of the threat, I started carrying a knife for protection between home and my martial arts training, as it made me feel safer.

Eventually I told one of my instructors about me carrying a knife and they suggested carrying a heavy metal pen because of the illegal nature of carrying a knife. So, for a period of three months I carried a knife and then a heavy metal pen for protection, whenever I walked alone from home to training and back. My decision to carry a knife for protection may not seem related to mental illness, however, upon reflection it was yet another sign of PTSD combined with the learned behaviours I had gained from growing up with my parental figures. For instance, one of my parents would always sleep with a knife under the bed and under the pillow.

Realisation and Appreciation of My Sister and Improved Relationship

During my childhood and until I was about 19, I would often start arguments with my sister, for my own amusement, and tease her every chance I had. The last time my sister and I had a large verbal argument it ended in a positive two-hour conversation. I had started an argument like I often would, and this particular day my sister replied with "maybe I look up to you". This stopped me in my verbal assault as I was not expecting a complement. We then sat down and talked, and it was during this conversation that I realised that most of my negativity, resentment and jealousy of my sister stemmed from my childhood.

We discussed how the various punishments I received from both parents, the protection our father gave her from our mother and the lack of abuse she received from him, and the punishments that directly profited her (such as my Christmas present being given to my sister as punishment to me) led to these negative emotions. The context of her being a child as well during these times, never entered my mind until this particular conversation.

After this conversation, our sibling relationship improved, and whilst I continue to tease her in jest;

there is no conscious malice or resentment in the insults or jokes directed to her. She knows that if she wants intelligent advice, that I am always willing to help.

NQ Martial Arts as Self-Medication

When I eventually returned to North Queensland my martial arts training increased. I dabbled in Mixed Martial Arts at one martial arts gym, Kickboxing at another, and eventually trained in Muay Thai, and Wing Chun Kung Fu at different martial arts schools. My training reached its peak during this time and I would often train up to eighteen hours a week in the various martial arts, despite working very physical jobs such as a butcher. I would often talk with people who were returning to training after ten years and could not understand how they let their martial arts training priorities fall.

When I met my eventual wife, my priorities would change for the better and I understood that there was more to life than martial arts. My conscious reason for training in martial arts was to challenge myself physically, and because I enjoyed being fit. However, when I look back and assess why I trained so much, it was an escape from spending time at home (as I was living with my mother again, after returning from Brisbane) and it was a great way to channel all my anger and trauma into something positive.

After meeting Paige, I would continue my martial arts training on the side; going on to dabble in Krav Maga,

Aiki Jiu-Jitsu and Goju-ryu Karate; train in Zen Do Kai; and then dabble in Brazilian Jiu-Jitsu and Aikido. I would do training and become a Tai Chi for health instructor at my first psychology job. The changing of martial arts styles was probably evidence that I was becoming disinterested in martial arts. I would later compete in several kickboxing fights with the support of Paige, prior to the birth of our first son.

Following the birth of our first son, I lost my mongrel and therefore found sparring difficult and lost interest in competing and training in martial arts. Looking for an external reason not to train I spoke to one of my martial arts instructors when he was busy, about my difficulty training and sparring. As he was busy, he gave me a neutral response which I used as the final reason to not return to training. I train casually in martial arts, but rarely if ever participate in sparring or competitions as my focus is more on my children rather than my martial arts ability.

19 +

More Focus on My Future Wife

I was training up to eighteen hours a week in various martial arts, while maintaining various jobs (from fast food to working as a butcher fifty hours a week). My predominant thought during and after work was about martial arts. I would occasionally have arguments with managers who would attempt to force me to stay back after my finish time (using the threat of less shifts); but because I chose to make my martial arts training a priority and I knew I was good at my job; these threats did not impact my decision making. Martial arts was my focus until I met a receptionist at one of the martial arts schools I was training at.

'Paige' would often collect my payment for the training, and then occasionally train in the cardio kickboxing class I would also train in. Until one day she dropped my money under the laptop, to which I wittily replied "smooth". Soon after this event Paige initiated our friendship outside the dojo; and asked, "what I was doing on the weekend". We met up socially on approximately two occasions, at several nightclubs. One of the nightclubs had an area for people over twenty-one-year-old, but as I was only nineteen, I was unable to go. My age then surprised Paige's friend who did not realise how young I was as Paige and her friend are four to five years older. I would later find out that Paige was the sister-in-law to the martial arts instructor and dojo owner; and that Paige asked this instructor to confirm I was over eighteen because of my 'baby face', as she thought I may have been sixteen. One of our first dates was a picnic at the local beach, which I later found out was not common for young people. One of Paige's work friends reportedly told Paige that there was a very strong chance I would one day propose because it was not normal for young people to do dates anymore. I would also eventually ask Paige to marry me at the same location as our first picnic date, using a CD player and a song by the band 'Train', known as 'Marry Me'.

After the romantic relationship became more long term, I discussed with James my "five-year plan". Originally my five-year-plan meant I would marry Paige after five years and propose in the five-year period. However, within three years I proposed, and we were married and built a house within my "five-year plan". I am not great with understanding my emotions but when asked, why I married Paige so quickly, I often answer that "it felt right".

Healing Begins

As well as my changing focus, something unexpected happened as a result of meeting Paige. Prior to meeting Paige, I would have nightmares daily, involving my childhood and my ability to defend myself. As my relationship with Paige became more serious, I also noticed my nightmares started to decrease, and eventually reduced to once a fortnight. My ability to care for a person increased and the ability to express my feelings in words improved. I also learnt a lot of social nuances from Paige, which helped me develop socially, emotionally, and professionally. This 'healing' and support from Paige would also lead to massive improvements in my self-awareness and self-confidence.

Whilst I had always been able to express myself through sarcasm, it wasn't until I met Paige, that I was able to be fully comfortable with who I was as a person, even if that meant embracing my differences. I was also then able to portray a level of confidence in situations where I was nervous, such as interviews or public speaking and share my opinion more often. Unfortunately, this increase in my self-confidence and the ability to embrace my differences led to several long-term friends distancing themselves and pretending, they did not know me when I attended a ten-year high school reunion. This was difficult to understand emotionally, especially as two of them had been at my wedding several years prior, but I was able to discuss this with Paige and move on.

I now embrace my difference and even use it as a tool in my professional life.

Since meeting Paige, I have felt that my life has been a lot easier. Whilst the lack of daily nightmares is a major positive, I also feel that other aspects of my life have become easier. My effort in life has been better directed and the outcomes attached to the effort have often been positive. I am not a spiritual person, so instead I look for another reason for this positive change of luck. I feel that Paige's support and care have allowed me to grow to be the best version of myself, no matter how weird that may be.

Study, Work and Mental Illness

When I was twenty, I decided to study again. I saw an advertisement for personal trainers and thought about my experience in martial arts. Paige was supportive and even though we did not have much money at the time, she still supported me travelling from North Queensland to Brisbane for the training. I eventually began working for her brother-in-law (my previous martial arts instructor) for close to eighteen months. My boss eventually moved his personal training business to the local university gym in NQ. After six months, he decided to combine his personal training and martial arts business into the one location, and I decided to return to university.

During my time as a personal trainer working with my wife's brother-in-law, I gained invaluable professional experience, which not only helped me start my own PT business on the side, but also teach me skills that were transferable in the mental health sector such as building rapport, being non-judgmental, goal setting and the interplay between physical and mental health.

Signs of my difference were once again highlighted when I had my twenty-first birthday party. I was involved in various social groups and ended up inviting eighty people to the party. I had told my mother and sister that for my twenty-first birthday present I wanted to have a party at the local beach volleyball centre, which also had a pool. I asked everyone invited if they could bring five dollars to the party instead of a present or alcohol for me, to help pay for the venue hire. Out of the eighty invited, I had thirty plus yes replies. The night of my party however, only one of the yes people attended and it was the least expected of the thirty. Thankfully, however, my party wasn't completely ruined as my sister's husband at the time had invited some of his friends whom I kind of knew already, and my wife, sister and mother were there, so we could still enjoy the night. I later found out that many of the people who had replied yes, did not attend as they had a better party offer that included free alcohol. This taught me some more life lessons about levels of connection such as the extreme difference between acquaintance and friends, and that I was indeed vastly different to my peers.

When I was twenty-one/twenty-two, Paige encouraged me to see a psychologist as we were talking about getting married and starting a family. There was a psychologist on campus at the university in North Queensland that I was attending, and an appointment was booked. I saw the university psychologist for several appointments and he then referred me to another psychologist who was in private practice. After several sessions with the new psychologist, I was eventually diagnosed with PTSD and Asperger Syndrome (which is now better known as ASD).

The psychologist also informed me it would be beneficial to have a brain scan (MRI) to rule out any brain damage that may have occurred from childhood abuse. The diagnoses were beneficial for me as it allowed me to understand why I acted and thought in particular ways and would eventually assist in my own professional career five years later.

When deciding what to study at university, I thought about what I was good at. I enjoyed exercise but was terrible at algebra (required for sport and exercise science degree); I enjoyed history but did not want to be a teacher (as being a teacher would be way too difficult). I then decided that since I like to help people help themselves, and was good at analysing behaviours, I would try psychology. So, I began my Bachelor of Psychology at the local university.

During the four and a half years of study – I worked three to four jobs often at the same time ranging from hospitality, adult retail, reception, and fitness; volunteered at the university and a mental health organisation; met several friends whom I still talk to either on social media or at fitness training; had knee surgery on both legs that led to minimal exercise for twelve weeks; I married Paige; studied a diploma of counselling at TAFE; built a house; and started my new family; graduating seven months after the birth of my first son.

Due to my choice to work up to four jobs while completing my Bachelor of Psychology and Diploma of Counselling, my social interaction lessened. This did not have much impact on me until my ten-year high school reunion. At my high school reunion, a total of fifty people from the original two hundred attended. On the night of the reunion, I tried to catchup with some of the friends that I had made at high school, and that I had caught up with a month prior to the reunion. The two who had attended my wedding and (one of whom was my high school formal partner), pretended that they did not know me or my wife. Ironically, the person who was the nicest to my wife and I was my high school ex-partner. My now former friends' response left me confused, so I stopped all contact with them, and even contacted a mutual friend Greta, to see if I had done something, or had missed something. Greta had no information or opinion to add.

Many years later, I saw the two former friends in a shopping centre, and attempted to be polite by saying hello, one pretended they did not see my wife or I by looking at their feet after they had made eye contact with me from a distance, and the other pretended not to see my wife or I by looking at the ceiling of the shopping centre. This time I was not confused and could only laugh at how some people's emotional maturity and need to hold onto a particular social standing impacted their ability to move forward.

When I was twenty-five it was confirmed that my lack of visual ability while awake was linked to a newly named mental disorder known as Aphantasia. While conscious I am unable to see or remember any type of imagery including colours, words, or objects, and am unable to explain what Paige or my family look like. This has no effect on my ability to recognise people, or changes in people when they are in front of me. However, it does impact my mood in unexpected ways. When I see photos of my loved ones, I have mixed emotions. I am happy to have my wife and kids in my life, but when I see their photo, I often become saddened as I am unable to remember what they looked like (and sometimes don't recognise old photos of my children).

The only theories regarding Aphantasia at present suggest that it is either a trauma response or linked to autism, which does not provide any clarity for myself as I have both diagnoses. However, more recent research is suggesting more and more that Aphantasia is a trauma response, and that the ASD link was only a correlation. This also suggests that people with ASD are more likely to receive trauma often from social situations.

When I was twenty-seven, I had a long period of dizziness with no observable trigger. So, after multiple visits to my local GP practice, I requested a brain scan to confirm if there was any brain damage from my childhood, or martial arts sparring. Thankfully, the results came back okay, and I was told by the neurologist that it is highly likely I have Mal de Debarquement Syndrome (or sea sickness on land) that was causing random dizziness. The neurologist told me that whilst there is no cure, it is not malignant, and I just had to monitor it. The MdDS diagnosis was also a positive as it ruled out any brain damage relating to childhood events, which lessened any anxiety relating to the fear of having this kind of brain damage.

Family History of Mental Illness and Trauma

As well as the direct family events that I have discussed, my family also has a long history of mental illness (most of it obvious but undiagnosed as my family until recently did not believe in mental illness). Both my parents had poor childhoods. One parent had abusive and neglectful parental figures and chose to be homeless from twelve years of age until they were between sixteen to seventeen, often choosing to live in graveyards to avoid family services. This parent's father was physically abusive towards his children and their mother (even killing an unborn child in the mother's stomach) and their mother was emotionally abusive and neglectful, often spending food money on Elvis Presley merchandise. The other parent experienced the negative effects of abusive parental figures and a faulty foster care system, including further abuse in this foster system, along with having obvious ASD symptoms throughout their childhood and as an adult.

My parents met when one was sixteen and the other twenty-nine, but whenever my sister and I asked how they met, the topic was always changed. This response led to speculation about how they met, considering the age of the older parent, and considering I was born approximately nine to ten months after they met. My parents took a lot longer than I to overcome their childhoods, and unfortunately for me it was not until I was about fifteen that they separated. Unfortunately for them, it was not until I was eighteen that my parents appeared to be managing their adult lives appropriately.

I have next to no contact with my extended family and I have been told I have approximately eight aunties and uncles and upwards of twenty cousins who I have never met. I have met both biological grandfathers – Dale who I discussed earlier; and my other grandfather who was racist and made my mother and I stand outside his house because we were "too black" for his wife. I have only met one of my biological grandmothers, and as a child we knew her only as "the old cow" and did not learn her name until many years later; and I attended the other grandmother's funeral when I was very young. As briefly mentioned earlier, Dale also has an unknown number of illegitimate children in Australia and overseas, that I have never met.

There was a family friend we called uncle who was in prison for the first thirteen years of my life, apparently for various robbery charges, but he disengaged once he finished his prison sentence. Originally, I did not understand why weren't allowed to see our "uncle", but years later I was told that he had inappropriate behaviours that my mother did not want us to witness or be involved in. The two aunties I do remember meeting have diagnosed schizophrenia, undiagnosed agoraphobia, and an intellectual disorder between them. From the cousins I have met, two of them are showing mental illness signs; and two of them have a history of drug and alcohol misuse from their own experiences of poor parental figures and the flawed child safety system in Australia. Thankfully, one of them appears to be functioning well on the outside and has managed to be a single parent for most of their parenting as well as hold down stable employment. My sister has told me that the other cousin with whom I am social media friends with is also doing well at present.

Almost all my adult family members have been divorced on multiple occasions due to poor communication skills and poor insight regarding their mental illness and triggers. Whilst divorce itself does not equal mental illness; the pattern of divorce my family has followed suggests that mental illness may have played a large part of their poor relationship choices.

I am very fortunate in many ways, that I cannot remember the first twelve years of life, as this means I rarely experience flashbacks while conscious, and when I am triggered, it is often only felt physiologically. Unfortunately, for my sister, she remembers the negative events that happened to me, the powerlessness she felt trying to protect me, as well as the negative events that she experienced from family and other people. This has led to her own personal struggles and ongoing mental health difficulties.

Memory and Processing Today

Today I am still impacted from my childhood and the combination of ASD and PTSD symptoms affect me in various ways.

The PTSD symptoms mean that I have multiple triggers which affect my perception of events such as perceiving potential danger in most social scenarios and preferring to sit in certain locations in a room for my perceived safety. I am triggered when I feel injustice towards myself and towards my family, despite how positive my life is today. I feel this is linked to the theme of injustice of my first fifteen years of life from my parents towards me and from various other events and people. I am great at processing information presented to me from clients or the environment but cannot remember the information 48 hours later unless they are written as session notes that I can refer to later. However, I can be triggered by the process of writing the client session notes if the client's presentation is too similar to my own childhood, or if the trauma information they share was unexpected.

I have constant muscle soreness from what is known as 'Hyper-arousal', which also lessens my tolerance for daily stressors and means I have almost constant muscle pain. I experience regular chest pain, sometimes leading to me needing to sit down, and do my own version of the stroke test. I have poor memory regarding any positive events in my life that involve people (interpersonal memory) such as my wedding, the birth of my children, what I did yesterday, etc. My ability to parent to the level I aim for is also impacted.

Lastly, I have a great interpersonal memory when I perceive that a person has slighted or wronged me which makes holding grudges much easier. To help explain to my children why I sometimes explode or respond verbally, beyond what is considered normal, I wrote a poem known as 'The Scars on my Brain'. To date my children sometimes refer me to this poem once I apologise for my verbal response. I have found this poem to be very helpful, as it gives my children a language, they can use to understand some of the aspects of my PTSD in an age-appropriate way, without having to understand complex mental illness. The poem in its entirety is provided at the end of this book in the 'Appendix' section.

An example of when my PTSD was triggered involved neighbour hood children at three pm on one afternoon. I was working as a personal trainer while at

university and had come home for an afternoon sleep. While asleep, my only child at the time was getting ready for bed. Normally my wife would have had my son in his cot at a specified time, but thankfully this day she was thirty minutes behind our normal schedule. As I was falling asleep, I heard a weird glass noise, but chose not to inspect the noise as I assumed it was our slow cooker making the noise.
Approximately five minutes later I heard it again, and by the time I had made it to the lounge room my wife was also inspecting the noise. When we investigated the noise further, we found a rock had smashed the front window of my son's bedroom, and another rock was in his cot.

This led to me feeling enraged, but I thought I would be able to put on a calm exterior, and I went door knocking. At three pm, in a 'Neighbour hood watch' area, on a busy corner, no one saw anything, or at least that is what I was told. When I returned home, my wife informed me that I did not look very calm. I then had difficulty sleeping for several weeks after, as any noise from outside woke me. Thankfully, my wife Paige supported my idea of buying security cameras, and once the cameras were installed, I was able to return to my normal sleep quality.

The ASD symptoms mean I sometimes misinterpret or miss subtle social or emotional cues which in my personal life have led to many minor arguments with my wife. I sometimes find it difficult to appreciate other perspectives in social and family situations, especially if their intellectual strength is in an area I don't care about. This has led to me calling my mother-in-law stupid (before I was studying psychology), which I felt was accurate at the time, but I now know is not socially acceptable. I also have difficulty speaking with my in-laws for extended periods of time as they don't challenge me intellectually as their strengths are in areas different to my own, so I become bored quickly. Occasionally when some of my in-laws share their opinions as facts which are overtly wrong, I have a very difficult time being silent and become verbally aggressive. I understand that my reaction is more a reflection of my want to help people improve and not my in-laws' responsibility. I am always working on trying to improve my response, albeit with limited success thus far.

I am able to put on different "hats" such as my professional hat which has some benefit but also means context greatly affects my perception of events. Lastly, I have a great memory recall for useless information such as facts, examples from movies, or statistics, except when I attend trivia nights where ironically, most of my useless information seems to disappear.

As well as the above, I feel that in recent years signs of ADHD have re-emerged that may be different to my ASD and PTSD symptoms, although having ASD and PTSD would make getting ADHD diagnosed very difficult. Hyper-focus and distractibility have increased my frustration and stress levels. The time spent with a psychologist that used a neuropsychology approach has highlighted that my brain may be similar to those with ADHD. However, as I do not want to take medication a diagnosis and treatment would not differ from what I am currently doing. It has also been suggested by professionals that I may have Alexithymia which in simple language means I don't understand my own emotional state, and instead rely on my physiological state.

Being a Psychologist with ASD and PTSD

Having PTSD and ASD does impact my practice as a psychologist, although the difficulties are not often noticeable to my clients or colleagues. As already discussed, there are some subtle social cues I can miss during a session with a client. This means I have to write more notes, leave myself questions to follow up on after the session, and rely more on behavioural changes and consistency of information the client provides me to ensure I am doing my best job to help the client.

Having difficulty understanding my own emotions means that it is harder for me to teach clients about emotions in a more natural way and means the depth of emotion I teach them may be less than some of my colleagues. Instead, I have overcome this difficulty by designing templates about almost every aspect of psychology I learn about. The templates then become a tool that the client can use to improve their own mental health, and additionally is also a tool I provide to my colleagues to streamline some of their practices.

My difficulty understanding emotions also means some mental illness indicators are more difficult for me to understand and notice, whereas other indicators are much more obvious to me. There are ten specific personality disorders according to the book we use in psychology known as the 'Diagnostic Statistics Manual fifth edition' (DSM-V). To overcome my weakness in this area, I have had to design a template for each of the personality disorders that I learn about, so I am more proficient at understanding and recognising their presentations. The mental illness presentations that I am above average at noticing include ASD, PTSD, ADHD and anxiety and depression, with other mental illness presentations being somewhere in the middle of my skill level.

Due to my poorer interpersonal memory for positive events and interactions, I rely a lot on my notes and templates when helping people, and when trying to understand the person's experience. This means I spend between ten to twenty-five minutes per client having to process and type out my handwritten notes, so that I can effectively consolidate the information and stories of the clients and work towards future planning with them.

This is okay when I have a quiet week, but when my work week is full, it means I have to spend extra time typing notes, which is unpaid time, so I can ensure I provide the quality the client deserves.

Having PTSD also means I have to work very hard to ensure my physical and psychological health is kept at a high level so that I am less triggered by client's presentations and experiences. I have to train (for me, in calisthenics, such as the Human Flag exercise) on a regular basis, eat a relatively healthy diet, and maintain a regular sleep routine (which can be hard with children under six-years-old). Whilst I have to work harder than some of my colleagues to remain mentally balanced, it does mean my lifestyle is healthier and more sustainable in the long-term.

Lastly, I recognise the amount of hard work I have done to enable myself to be successful in life. As a result, I do not consume any alcohol. There are obvious positives of this: better health, more money in the bank, etc.

However, the real reason I do not consume any alcohol is because I fear how the drunk version of me may behave. I worry that my aggressive childhood, my martial arts backgrounds combined with the lack of inhibitions may make me become physically aggressive. I also worry that if I was to drink I would have even less social filter than I currently do, and say things that are hurtful, just because the inebriated me may feel they are the truth. For me, the benefits of not consuming alcohol are far greater than using alcohol or any other substance.

I also manage the number and quantity of stimulants such as tea I consume as I do not want to increase my difficulties with managing my emotions. I also want to ensure the best version of myself my maintaining as much control of myself as possible.

Identifying Positives thus far

By this part of the story, I have mainly focused on many negative events that I experienced which makes it easier to feel exhausted. However, I also hope that by this point the many positive events and experiences discussed are also appreciated and understood. Firstly, my nightmares decreased from daily to fortnightly when I met Paige. I am glad to share, that since the birth of my first son my nightmares decreased from fortnightly to approximately monthly to two monthly, and even when they occur, they have less impact on my functioning than they did previously.

Secondly my focus changed from martial arts, to Paige and my sons, and I also improved my ability to care and empathise. The first event I use to demonstrate this increase in empathy is the night my first son had his first nightmare. He was in his cot, and I woke to him crying in his sleep. I turned to Paige and told her how I had chest pain, which was different to the chest pain I have felt from the PTSD, heart murmur or previous sporting injury. She looked at me with a smile and said, "that is caring". It was the first time I had ever felt that level of emotional connection, and whilst I did not like the feeling of the chest pain, I was glad to have an emotional connection with my child.

Following the birth of my other children, nightmares involving my childhood, continued to lessen dramatically, and when I do have negative dreams, their content is more to do with parenting and relationships than flashbacks of trauma. I feel this demonstrates how much my PTSD symptoms have improved, although there is still a lot of improvement left. Further to this, my sense of empathy has improved. I often joke that this is a bad thing as it means I have lost my ability to activate my 'mongrel' when I want to, which was very useful during my martial arts training, and since losing this ability, I perceive my martial skill as only average at best. Even though my focus has shifted to my new family, I still maintain a hobby which is predominately calisthenics as part of my 'self-care'.

Next, my relationship with my sister has improved. My sister understands that whilst I may not have the same level of connection with her that other siblings may have, the fact that she is on the list of people I care about is a big step. She also has discussed with Paige and I that she understands I care about her, and that I have difficulty saying so in person.

Next my self-awareness has greatly improved as I believe I have a greater understanding regarding my emotions, thoughts, symptoms, weaknesses, and strengths, and this continues to improve personally and professionally. As I was fortunate enough to be able to break any possible cyclic behaviour patterns that existed; I am now of the opinion that cyclic behaviour is only a predisposition to poor behaviour and poor life choices, and not an excuse that some individuals or groups tend to use. I also understand that cyclic behaviour makes it exceedingly difficult to make positive life choices, but it is possible to break the cycle and that breaking the cycle is easier with support. I believe that ignorance was once a haven for me during childhood, but self-awareness has become a strength for me as an adult.

Next, I am proud to be the first in my family to complete high school in one attempt, and the first to complete a Certificate three and four, a Diploma, and a Bachelor's degree.

Lastly, I had the realisation that my parents did their best. This is not to excuse them of the many years of wrongdoing; but an attempt to understand why they chose certain behaviours as parents. As odd as it seems, I believe that most of the negative experiences mentioned in this book came from a place of caring. My parents had no positive role models, poor self-awareness, no understanding of mental health, traumatic childhoods of their own, almost no assistance in parenting, poor communication skills, negative learnt behaviours and the almost constant external stressor of low income.

I have told both parents how I have diagnosed PTSD linked to fifteen years of abuse and my mother cried and apologised. My father stated that he "couldn't remember any parenting mistakes and he is now a Buddhist". My father's response was unsurprising, but it did make me angry at him as I saw this conversation as an opportunity for him to apologise. I currently only talk with my parents when my wife or sister encourage me to do so, or when I want something from them or for my children's events such as birthdays etc. Giving credit where it is due, when I do want something and ask my parents for help such as babysitting, teaching my child another language or concreting, they are often now available.

Even with my attempt at understanding my parents' behaviours; I strongly believe that without the previously mentioned support of James and his family; Mat and his family; Margaret and her family; my sister, and Paige; my parents' best would not have been enough for me to still be alive today. These supportive people have helped so much as they demonstrated what positive role models were to me and helped to teach me the positive moral values that I continue to use today.

Looking towards the future
<u>Barriers only slow us down</u>
Since meeting Paige my life has improved greatly. Despite this, I have still had to overcome several obstacles. Compared to my childhood these obstacles were not massive but were still large enough to impact my mental health.

My first New Year's Eve with Paige I was hospitalised. I was working as a butcher which required me to go from the fridge area to the hot summer weather outside. I went home early on New Year's Eve as I was feeling unwell and dehydrated. Paige took me back to my mother's house where I was living and ran me a bath. The room temperature water caused me severe pain, so Paige took me to the hospital. I then spent the next twenty-four hours in hospital and received multiple Saline bags. The week of the following New Year's I gave Paige my shirt as she was cold, and it was raining. The following day I was again hospitalised and again received multiple Saline bags to rehydrate me. I feel that Paige's assistance during both times was a positive indicator of her positive qualities and demonstrated the kind of caring person she is.

Earlier I discussed how Paige supported me with my personal training aspirations. I saw this as very positive, but the unexpected negative meant I now had to find the motivation to improve myself and life internally. Paige did and still does care for me unconditionally, which is great, but also means any change I make, has to be for me. I have always been driven but also had the finance or the fear of my parents as background external motivators when my internal motivation waned. I eventually found the internal motivation to finish my personal training certificate three and four, but it took me twelve months instead of twelve weeks to complete.

I started university at North Queensland in semester two and started with two subjects instead of the normal four subjects. Unfortunately for me, I required knee surgery on both of my knees four week before my final exams of the semester. One of my lecturers was happy for me to sit a deferred exam since I could not walk. However, the head of department for psychology did not sign off on a deferred exam for one of the psychology exams as he did not think that not having the ability to walk was a good enough reason for missing an exam. Whilst this put my university back a small amount, I was able to find a way to get some time back by completing a subject over the following summer holiday period.

I previously mentioned that during my university years in North Queensland, I had worked many jobs. One of my jobs was at an adult retail store. A gym friend knew I was looking for an extra job to help pay the bills and he told me of a position that was vacant. I knew almost nothing of the adult industry but knew the owner (also from the local gym) so I applied and was successful. Several months later the owner sold the business, and the new owner hired a manager to work for him.

The manager seemed like a nice person, proactive, and eventually seemed trustworthy. She paid me in cash each week and told me that the boss wanted the tax taken out for the books. I worked there for several months, and then left due to other commitments. When tax time came, and I received my Pay-G tax slip and it showed that I had paid almost no tax. When I queried this with the boss, he told me that the manager had been stealing money from myself and him and that she was uncontactable and that the police had been notified. From this experience, I learnt to never trust another employer again, regardless of how nice they seemed; and that any agreement or request from or for my manager always had an email or paper trail to protect myself.

After I graduated from university, the mental health company I had been volunteering for advertised a job. I knew the area manager of the company (from my volunteering) which helped in the interview, and I was successful in the interview. I enjoyed my first six months there, and when my team leader left, the job became even more enjoyable.

However, when they appointed a new team leader three months later, the enjoyment at work lessened. The new leader was a nice person but came from the public mental health system and tried to instigate those practices in the community mental health sector, albeit with some success. After voicing several frustrations, my team leader suggested that I think about working in a different area of psychology, which I internally took great offence to. Unfortunately, several weeks later when voicing similar frustrations to my primary psychology supervisor, she also suggested I think about working in a different area of psychology. This led to me eating lunch outside so I could escape the work environment.

The community mental health company I worked for had been working closely with another mental health provider, often referred to as the "sister organisation". After about twelve months of working, the two organisations "merged", or more accurately the "sister organisation" took over the company I was working for. This was a short term positive, as it meant we all received pay increases.

However, the new manager quickly started making changes and within three months, many people were offered redundancies, were "encouraged to leave" or were fired. As a provisional psychologist at this time, I was very concerned about the health of my clients due to the team all finishing up, so I added a caveat to all of my client's files to protect myself professionally.

The new manager hired a "professional" from Brisbane, officially to learn the ropes, but in reality, the professional's role was to read through all of our notes. When they found my caveat, I was encouraged to leave, but was able to push for a month extension to complete all my notes. I then had to apply for another job, which thankfully came quickly, with Headspace accepting my application. As a provisional psychologist changing jobs, and supervisors, I had a large amount of paperwork I had to get approved, and had to take a large pay cut, but was grateful to have a job.

The final difficulty I experienced in my journey to become a generally registered psychologist happened over a five-day period. I took three years and one day to complete my internship, and unknown to me the governing body had changed the policy. The original policy provided five years to complete your internship, with a letter being required after three. However, by the time I got to three years, the new policy was for me to reapply for a provisional psychology role. So, on Thursday I was told I would receive a phone call regarding my registration. However, on the Friday I was told I was deregistered. Upon hearing this news, I cried in my office as I thought this meant I would lose my job, and I was stressed about how I was to provide for my wife and son.

After getting the courage to see my team leader, I told them what was happening, and they were very supportive. Over the weekend my wife and I stressed about finances, and my career. The following Monday I finally received authorisation to become a "provisionally provisional psychologist". On the Tuesday I was then emailed and told that they had received and marked my final assessment and that I was now a generally registered psychologist. Thankfully for me, my wife and my team leader were supportive. I feel that being forced to leave my first psychology job became a massive positive, because the Headspace team leader, and the two primary psychology supervisors that I had at Headspace were very supportive, and helped me grow as a psychologist, even suggesting I had a strong future in counselling psychology.

I feel that the governing body above psychology needs to do a better job in their dealings with provisional psychologists instead of seeing them as only numbers. Thankfully, my story had a happy ending, but this may not always be the case if the governing body does not improve.

My last example focuses on a large book company in Australia. My previous version of this memoir was sold online through amazon by myself. Six months later when I was searching for a book online, I saw that a well-established and very popular book store was selling my memoir without my permission. Someone in their company had stolen a copy of my memoir and was selling on their online only store. I then contacted them and provided evidence I was the author. Thankfully they then removed it, but no apology or reimbursement was offered.

My Parenting

As mentioned, I have various difficulties stemming from my childhood and subsequent PTSD, my ASD as well as the slight disadvantages from my Aphantasia. I have also touched on my triggers and how they impact me. Parenting for me is difficult, like it is for most people, but I feel there are some areas that I find easier than other people and other areas that I struggle with a lot more than most people.

Firstly, I find the logical side of parenting relatively easy. When my children have questions about the world, I am often able to assist with appropriate and factual answers, when my children have questions about religion and I am able to answer these with facts whilst also leaving room for them to explore their own spirituality if they choose and I am also able to teach them physical and academic aspects about life, drawing from first-hand experience.

However, I find it very difficult when it comes to perhaps the most important part of parenting, emotions. I have developed and printed various emotion related posters and displayed these around the house, and these have assisted my sons and myself somewhat, but not to the extent I had originally hoped. When my children have difficulty with their emotions such as when they are incredibly angry, I try my best not to repeat my parents' response and try and calm them.

However, the times this does not work, I become triggered for multiple reasons – firstly I feel helpless that I cannot help them, secondly, I feel a sense of rejection that in the moment I have invested a great deal of effort for no positive outcome, and lastly my childhood is triggered and memories and stories from my childhood are reexperienced. I am still unhappy with the level of fear tactics I use when I parent which often involve glaring at my young children when they do not listen or yelling to make them pay more attention. Comparatively to my childhood, this may sound like nothing, but it does not fit well with my goal of not repeating my parents' mistakes.

One parental example when I was not able to manage my own emotions involved my then two-year-old. He was having a difficult day and was not listening and was unsure what he wanted. In reaction to this I struggled to understand what he wanted which led to me yelling. In reaction my yelling my son then became angry and aggressive himself and did not want to see me. After about thirty or so minutes of no progress for either myself or my son, I became whelmed and had to leave the house and go for a drive. My son then screamed as he wanted me to stay, but I could not manage my own emotions or his. So, I left, not knowing where I was going to go, and ended parking at the nearest shopping centre to calm. Several days later, my wife told me that she had the fear that I would drive off and never return, because of the stories and movies she had seen.

Despite my parental short-comings, I feel that my level of effort and want to continue to improve as a person and parent will assist me greatly in helping my children grow.

One example of where my childhood has impacted my parenting is when my oldest son was bullied at school. After spending two weeks helping build my son's confidence to participate in the school's 'Running Club', my son was bullied. While I was watching for the first time (I previously had to run with him), my son's peer pushed my son over on five occasions in the first lap. My instinct was to "deal with the child", but I listened to my psychology brain and what my wife would say, and instead wrote an email to my son's teacher explaining not only what had happened but how I felt about the situation. The teacher was able to provide me with a satisfactory response.

I feel that there will be many more difficult situations where one of my children are bullied at school. However, as a parent who is trying my best to teach my children the socially acceptable way to respond, I feel I must continue to listen to my wife, and my psychology brain, so I don't repeat my parent's behaviours.

I am also extremely fortunate that when I am struggling emotionally, my wife Paige is able to assist me by offering me a brief idea, by stepping in and taking over or by saying our parental safe phrase of 'Shark Music'.

Moving Forward

I thought I was managing my PTSD symptoms effectively. However, when my third child was born, I realised that there was still more work I needed to do for my mental health.

My anger was not as well-managed as I had thought, and my yelling were not proportional to the stimulus. This then led to self-judgment and fear that I would repeat my parents' mistakes. Occasionally this fear would lead me to cry, until my wife was able to reassure me that I wasn't like my parents.

This new insight regarding how much work I still had left to do, led me to start searching for a new psychologist. When searching for a psychologist, I had to find someone, whom I felt would have more experience than me in mental health, be more intelligent on the areas that I excel in and have an approach that was not talk/emotion based. With help from my previous psychology supervisor, I chose a psychologist who took a neurobiological approach to treating PTSD.

Prior to my first session, I sent the psychologist a copy of my second draft of this memoir so they would have most of the background information. Following an introduction session and an unsuccessful attempt at EMDR, we began the neurobiological approach. This entailed me to watch a screen while wearing special equipment on my head, while the psychologist changed specific brain wave frequencies. As well as this during session, I also had "homework" that I was tasked with completing, including TRE (tension and trauma release exercises), BLS (bilateral stimulation via audio) and the 'Safe and Sound Protocol' (a special audio program). At first the TRE and BLS felt a bit "left wing" for my science type thinking, but I wanted to improve my management of the PTSD symptoms, so I was able to persevere. To date the most useful from the sessions was the 'Safe and Sound Protocol' as it was easy to do, and forced me to have time doing nothing. After several sessions the psychologist suggested her approach was ineffective due to the competing brain waves and symptoms, I am experiencing combined with my inability to access emotions in session.

This extra unexpected recovery journey highlighted the importance of maintenance of my health, and further supported what I already tell my clients.

My life motto is "just be great", which I often use sarcastically in social situations but also try to follow when I can. I believe that people should always strive to be the best version of themselves, which I try to do on a daily basis. When I fail to be the best version of myself, such as when I yell more than I should as a parent, I try to resolve the situation and try to learn from the mistake. I still have the positive values of hard work and respect that my parents taught me and continue to develop the values of family and caring that I have learnt from the people whom I have found most supportive. If I am working too much, my wife Paige will remind me, and her favourite saying is "kids want your presence, not your presents".

When life got too difficult, several things kept me going. Firstly, having a hobby which for me was martial arts and fitness. I currently train at my home gym three to five times a week and have several friends visit to train with me as my external motivation. Next, meeting someone who likes me for me was a massive help. Having the confidence to be my most honest self and embrace my oddities has improved my self-image and life.

Next having other people help me, often without me realising. As mentioned in this memoir, I have had support along the way, and I believe that everyone can benefit from having at least one support person available or alongside them. Lastly acknowledging I needed help and having the courage to ask for help when I needed it. Asking for help from my friend James when I had suicidal ideation was a largely reaffirming and positive experience. Again, I feel that I am alive today because of James' response to my phone call when I was younger and his offering of help when I needed it prior and since the phone call. And then, with the help of my wife, asking professionals for help and being able to discuss my childhood openly and honestly, assisted in my personal and mental health growth and understanding.

Various Discriminations

I have chosen to add this section at the back of my memoir due to various people asking about specific discriminations I may have experienced in my life. I have included several although, some were more impactful than others. Throughout other sections of this memoir, I referred to some of the following discriminations, but I thought this would make it easier for future readers to have this very specific question answered.

Skin Colour – When I was approximately six years old, my family visited my paternal grandfather's house. My father and sister were allowed to enter the house. However, my mother and I had darker skin and were forced to stay outside for being "too black" for the paternal grandfather's wife.

Last Name – At the end of year six, I applied for school captain. After the voting was completed, it was announced that I had been chosen as school vice-captain. However, the teachers at the small-town school were not happy with this as their children did not hold any leadership positions, so a "recount" was held. Following this "recount" all the teacher's children and children who had particular last names, held leadership positions and I did not.

Less favoured – despite the rich neighbours giving me opportunities to earn money, it felt like they still preferred my sister. This became more evident when I was playing the trumpet at school. I lessened my practice hours and my sister started playing trumpet around this time. To help my sister improve, the neighbours bought my sister a trumpet of her own and then later a guitar.

Height – In year eight and nine, my HPE teacher favoured tall students, which became evident during our volleyball module. My friend who was six foot three inches did next to nothing during this module and received an A grade for his efforts, much to his and others' surprise. However, I enjoyed the sport so put a lot of effort into the module, jumping everywhere without care for my injury risk, and I received a C grade. When my tall friend and I queried this, it was ignored and the C grade was kept.

Country vs City – During the enrolment process before term four of year nine, the administration of my new city school made it very clear to me (in person) that they believed my A grades that I had earnt in a country high school were only worth a C in their school. This led me to not trying in schooling again until I failed a subject at university nine years later.

Income/Class – In year ten at my high school, we had an English assessment. I completed mine of the only paper my family had, which was foolscap sized. Instead of focusing on the content of my assessment, my English teacher thought it was appropriate to make fun of me for using the wrong sized paper.

I chose to only include one example of each direct discrimination, and not include any subtle or non-direct discrimination examples. I felt that including the non-direct and subtle types would sound like me ranting and take away from the journey I have had. I have been able to uses these experiences and my current position in life to assert myself when I feel discriminated against.

Memoir Close

Hopefully, this memoir has been an interesting and overall positive experience for you. I also hope that the negatives discussed can be used to help better understand the many positives that can arise from life's trials and tribulations, such as resilience and understanding.

If you are having difficulties, you will be surprised to find out how many people are available to listen or try to understand, despite how alone you may feel.

Part 2 – My Memoir as told via a factual but artistic lens (poem)

<u>Preface</u>

During my time volunteering for a mental health organisation in the community
I was told that the sharing of my story
To high school and university student looking at me
Helped them to understand the personal side of mental health
Which helped them improve their knowledge wealth
Of my diagnoses of ASD and PTSD
Ending in them asking questions of me

As a psychologist many young people have expressed
Their own experiences of distress
That led to their own difficulties such as feeling isolated and depressed
So I hope my artistic attempt of translating my memoir into a poem
Will help people feel comfortable talking with people who are supportive of them
For me this including my wife, friend's families and my best mate
Who I continue to be thankful for to this date

About Me
I was born in Mackay where I lived for several years until then
My family moved to a country town near Brisbane
I lived with my mother, father and sister
And despite my family working hard we didn't get far
When we left and sold the house, we didn't have much money left over
Where we lived with my aunty, her husband and my cousin which was very far
From the people I knew and friends I had made
But we needed to move as my father's injury meant we he was getting paid

My first twelve years of life memory
I am unable to remember so it has been told to me
By my sister, parents, and friends close to me
I have poor interpersonal memory in general and especially
For any positive experiences that happen to me
However, despite how hard I try to improve I unfortunately
Have a great memory
For any negative events of when I feel people have wronged me

I have had various behavioural issues mostly involving anger
Most probably as a result of fifteen years of abuse from my parents and other
And despite the many negative events, discussed in the memoir
I feel I was fortunate and have come far
I feel I have an advantage over some of my peers
And feel that I am older despite my lack of years
I current work as a psychologist and personal trainer
And continue to be in contact with the people who have helped shape me for the better

Aggressive Behaviours
During my primary school years
I was physically aggressive towards objects and my peers
I once slammed a student into a tap head first
And unfortunately that wasn't even the worse
Other times I threw kids into tables and chairs
Or when bullied by older kids, I threw one down the stairs
I was bullied at primary schools one then two
Where I had to constantly protect myself from bullies who
Would attack me in groups or alone
And I would have to explain this to my parents when I got home

The most extreme event involved me being hung over a bridge over the train track
So my mother had a conversation with their guardian, so they wouldn't attack
Me again
As I walked alone most days without any friends
Following this, I was then walked home from school for several days
And the kids weren't seen again, at least when we went home that way

My mother had a reputation at any school I attended
For being aggressive towards teachers, which she pretended
Was normal and okay
Which now I know is not the right way

My aggression did stop at being aimed at my peers
My sister who was younger by two years
Was an easy target for my pent-up anger
And I thought it was okay to verbally or physically attack her
Until one day when I punched her several times in the car
My parents physically attacked me, so I would never again go that far

For many years I wondered why no teachers or other adults stopped my parents' behaviours
And why for most of my childhood I had no other adult act as a saviour
But now I know it is because of the time and town
And that mental health knowledge was not around

Chores and Responsibilities
Chores were a regular part of life
And from the age of five
I would feed the animals, get ready for school and complete other tasks
But if they were not done exactly how my parents had asked
Various punishments including physical were used
But I had no idea this counted as being abused
My nights before bed included
Various tasks such as washing dishes with no dish excluded
If the dishes were not done the particular way that was demanded
A finish time of 10pm would become standard

Despite having asthma, my sister had it worse than me
Which meant she not forced to do as many tasks as far as I could see
I had to make her school lunch and bed even when
She was as old as I had been
And she wasn't forced to start until she was about eleven
This and many other examples led me to have triggers today

So when I feel someone is not "pulling their weight"
for a task or during a day
I become triggered more than I should
And react verbally more than most would

When I was young my mother had her legs operated on
And as I was her oldest child and son
The responsibility of the family shop
Fell to me, and on my BMX, I would hop
I would take the cash and my math brain
And carry the fortnight's shopping, in sun or in rain
As an adult, my former teacher reminded me
That she saw me carrying shopping on my bike and on my knees

Growing up in a town with no sewerage and just a septic tank
Meant I was needed to help clean it, and move compost, despite how it stank
When I was twelve, I moved too much compost at one time
And after I was punished, I was showered because of the smell and food slime

Silent Abuse – Verbal, Emotional and Physical
In my early years I was very logical
The first book I read my self was an encyclopedia, 600 pages in all
My logic was a great thing to have as a young kid
But led me to understand the flaws in arguments and behaviours my parents did
Where instead of being a positive it led to physical and emotion pain
And my parents had difficulties with the physical refrain

The most common form of abuse I received was verbal
Which was better than the physical/nonverbal
When I wasn't being yelled at, I was accused
Of Stealing a toy I was playing with, leading to physical abuse
The fact my parents thought me a liar
Led to other negative behaviours going higher

At school I couldn't blend in, and stood out instead
And after I was accused of stealing I stole money of my parents' cash reserve from under their bed
I used the money to try and buy friends
Which never worked out in the end
Also during primary school

There was a book from Book-Club that I thought was cool
So after saving my parents bought it for me
And when I received I was filled with glee
But like most of my positive events this ended in tears
As my parents felt I had ripped them off, and then parented using fear
Years later I got the book back from my mother
And because of the emotional journey the book still felt like no other
I have kept it as one of my favourite books
Even though if you were to stop and take a look
You would see it is written for kids
But the book is now more important because of what my parents did

When I was young we had an older kid live with us
Whose own childhood was not great and thus
Didn't know how to treat me in a positive way
Which led to a specific event happening one day
I was washing the dishes like normal and was complaining about it
And to help my mother out, the kid thought for a bit
And decided to stand with all of his weight
On top of my foot until it did break
I screamed in pain and my mother ran up from

downstairs
And for a moment I was relieved because if thought that she would care
But instead of saving me and punishing the other child
My mother grew angry and went wild
My mother used her parenting that she often used
And I was physically punished and abused
Because despite the amount of tears streaming
From my eyes and my screaming
I should have known better to complain
And just do the dishes as the older had been saying

Now as an adult if I injure myself
And my wife doesn't reply with her emotional wealth
I become triggered and react disproportionally
And withdraw or act angrily
But once I calm down, I know the fault isn't my wife
It is the experiences from earlier in life

Some examples of non-traditional abuse
Included sour food and even one kilogram of plums that were used
One more regular weird type of night time punishment
Involved me being forced to stand at the end of my parents' bed
And if my mother awoke and I had fallen asleep

I was physically punished and sometimes allowed to go to my bed to sleep

During the day if I back-chatted or swore
I would have to eat soap or hold diced chilli in my mouth and more
Would be added if I swallowed and the went
Down my throat, as the holding of chilli was seen as a fair punishment
When my behaviour with a toy was not seen as okay
My toys were smashed, cut up or given away
Often given to my sister as punishment to me
Leading to further resentment towards my younger sister, even though she
Was also a child and it wasn't her fault
The negative emotion went into a metaphorical vault
To help me catch five hundred gram jars were thrown at me
That were often filled with coffee
If I dropped them I would have to pay
So I learnt to catch very quickly, almost straight away

As a child when my pet guinea pig died
Instead of helping me with my loss as I had cried
I was told in graphic detail through my mother's usual shout
That the animal had died from the inside out

And that it was my fault for not filling its food and water too
Because as a child my mother thought I knew
How to look after an animal that was my responsibility
And as always, the blame fell on me

When we would for long drives that lasted days and nights
I would sleep during the day to avoid the light
When I awoke during the night and asked for food
I would get into trouble for being rude
Because sleeping through the day
Was seen by my parents as another way
Of be demonstrating that I was being poorly behaved that day

If as a child I was sick and vomited
Not in the sink but instead in my bed
Before helping me clean the mess
I was punished for my behavioural choice putting my parents' patience to the test

The final type of punishment was physical
With the main form involving smacking with hand, belt but that's not all
I would be slapped on the face, or thrown into a door down the hall

If I dodged a slap or spoke back, there would be more
And my mother had many belts kept in a drawer
My father preferred the to pick me up by the ear
To help with throwing me, landing on my rear

Despite all discussed and all that may follow
I feel my parents did their best as they could not borrow
From any positive parenting as they had none
So the methods they pulled from were the ones that were done

I felt as a child that fear meant respect
So still as a parent today I subconsciously expect
My children to do as they are told
Despite my children not being very old
As I will discuss later during this text discussing parenting pain
I have to work very hard to activate and maintain
My positive thinking part instead of my emotional brain

Low Income Family and our Neighbours
When I was still but a baby
My parents briefly lived with my aunty
Who also had a child thirteen days younger than me
And stress was high as there was minimal money
One example included my adult mother attacking her sister
With a doubled ended pencil, but instead she stabbed her
Own hand and if that wasn't bad enough, she was then
Hit by her mother 'The Old Cow' across the head with a pan

After moving to near Brisbane, we were able
To live in the same house which was quite stable
There were some occasions where my mother would without food
To keep my sister and I fed and clothed so we were never nude
And on occasions when a program run by the government
We would swap our ten dollars for a box of food and home we then went

In our earliest years my sister and I
Were given small change as pocket money for us to

save to buy
Things we may want but then our financial situation did change
So the spare five cent pieces were given as my mother had arranged
Despite our young age when our parents needed our pocket money back, we knew
That our parents' IOU
Meant they wanted to help us but couldn't
So my sister and I lessen the amounts they owed without their knowledge so they wouldn't
Feel as bad taking money back off of us
And we never told them, and never made a fuss

Before I was twelve, my mother, sister and I would walk the streets
Collecting aluminium metal, and cans so we had more money to eat
When I turned twelve, I started paid work
Digging potatoes, and working for our rich neighbour, which allowed me some perks
Also around this time, my aunty and cousins lived nearby
So I had twelve months of emotional escape whenever I wanted to say hi

Later I had my maternal grandfather for two years live next door
Which may have had positives, but I don't remember them anymore
I remember he was stern and would remind us of his military days
And was often very critical, even if it came from a positive place
He once attended my competing to which he
Told me how bad I was compared to him when he competed in the British military
After hand writing his own memoir
He asked that our mother
Type it up for him
And in all the text he only mentioned the one child important to him
His Caucasian son
He left out my mother, her two sisters and his illegitimate children

Strength in Academic Pursuit and Sporting Achievements

One way I found to enjoy life and function
Was my thirst for knowledge and competition
Despite being constantly bullied or kids attacking me
School was a welcome escape from home where I thrived academically
I was often in the top two in any class I was in
With my biggest downfall being my writing

Politics has followed me since childhood
With a major example from school that did not feel that good
I was elected by peers as a primary school vice-captain
But as the teacher's own kids were unsuccessful, they did the count again
Following the recount I lost my position
And this led me to never trying for a leadership position again
I received many awards for the various sports
Including aged champion for ruby league and athletics which led to a feeling of great import
Later, in high school I would find karate
And again I did very well, as it suited me

Early signs of an ASD brain
Whilst I have religion or religious belief now
When I was younger I attended Sunday School, and was confused how
A magical being could be my father
And when I went home and asked my mother
This led my Atheist mother to demonstrate anger
Another example involved inviting a friend over to listen to CD's
And when I chose the hits of the eighties
That was enjoyable to me
My mother pulled me aside and told me angrily
That if I listened to songs like macarena my friend would not want to speak with me
As they would think I was gay
Which for some reason would not have been okay

Ignorance and Sarcasm
I believe the saying "ignorance is bliss" was pertinent to me
As I did not understand the negatives I was experiencing and therefore could not see
That certain behaviours and events aimed my way
Would impact me to the level that they do today

Mental health topics were often unspoken, unknown or taboo
So if I ever had negative thoughts or thoughts to die, I never had the language to
Express these to another
Friend or family member such as my mother
In my town and my family
What was often told to me
Was you either ate concrete and just kept at it
Or you were "crazy" like my mother's aunty and would be in a straight jacket

Sarcasm was my favourite tool
To use whether at home or at school
It helped lessen any negative event
And way my negative emotions often went
Another positive about being known as intelligent and sarcastic
Is even when I am wrong, people think I am being

sarcastic
Which becomes even more fantastic

First Signs of Mental Illness, Misdiagnosed, and then Ignored by Parents

At seven years of age the local doctor gave me a mental health diagnosis
Which was ignored by parents, and thankfully has turned out to be the wrong primary prognosis
As an adult I would eventually be given a more accurate diagnosis
Of Asperger Syndrome, now ASD and Post-Traumatic Stress Disorder
And I have symptoms of ADHD, right near the border

The ASD was evident when our dog Lassie died
And I could see that my father had cried
I also knew about our lack of money
So with my logic brain, and not trying to be funny
I pointed out that we would save money on dog food
And was immediately physically punished for being inconsiderate and rude

During my school years my undiagnosed ASD
Meant most academic tasks were easy for me
I was very fortunate and therefore lucky
That the majority of my teachers supported me
With extra work from more senior books
Which I enjoyed and would often complete or have a look

Unknown Support Person

Despite my behaviours towards her
Unknown to me my main support person was my sister
Because of parental choices from my parents
Such as giving my sister my presents
I never stopped to think about how
Any of her behaviours helped me until now
When I wasn't in the room or was not near
She would stand up to bullies, or my parents when I couldn't hear

James and My Loss of Memory Pre-Twelve
At my local high school in year eight
I made a small group of friends that were quite great
From this group I met my best friend
Who I still talk with to this end
After I had known James for a year or so
My parents allowed me to go
And sleep over for the night until the next day
Where I started to learn that my "normal" was not okay
I was confused when James' parents weren't yelling and arguing
As I had grown up listening to bluing
I had grown to believe
That married people mostly hated each other without reprieve
But watching James' parents interact
Started to teach me how to act
I didn't realise this at the time
But still understood James' parents' behaviours were better than mine

Many years later I spoke with my best mate
When I was round twenty-eight
That I could not remember any events prior to
Twelve years of age, which allowed me to

Not be able to access all of the memories that were bad
But also meant I could experience or remember the glad
James informed me that as a kid
I often told him my negative experiences, despite the fact I hid
My emotions before I got to school
As I didn't want my peers to see me crying and think me even less cool

Due to this loss of memory or memory block
My earliest memory is at twelve even though I've tried a lot
To remember any good or bad
Prior to this age, which can make me sad
When talking with people today
When they reminisce or say
Their favourite memories or times
Especially when they ask me mine
As today I still cannot remember any positive memory
From any time in my life or any positive event that has happened to me
I cannot even remember my wedding with my wife
Nor the birth of my sons who in my life

Are the most important people to me
Followed by the importance I hold for my own library

There are two theories that explain why
When other's talk about their good childhoods, I cry
Because of the loss of memory
And these theories include my diagnosed ASD and PTSD
The PTSD theory discusses
How a person's brain can block memories when they hurt us
While ASD theory looks at how
My brain considers interpersonal memories less important from then and now

First Paid Jobs

Hard work was and still is one of my core values
And while you're still reading, let me tell you
How my first paid job at twelve which led to an internal celebration
Later found out that the neighbours paying me $1 an hour for digging food by hand was child exploitation
My next two jobs paid much better
Which allowed me to save and collect Star Wars information from the local newsletter

High School Achievements and Supportive People

During my almost two years at my first high school
I continued my habit of not being very cool
But achieved well academically
Including being enrolled in an advanced subjects, and entering competitions which was great for me
I also started my first martial art in Karate
That was run by the science teacher we called Mr. B
And I enjoyed that training, for my mind and body
My science teacher and German subject teacher assisted me
With extra Karate trainings in Brisbane, fees, and even a Gi
On Thursday nights on the way home after training
My German subject teacher would stop by her mother's house even if it was raining
I was then given a bag of the day's bread from the bakery
That I was able to take home for my family
I would go on to win various karate events including solo and as part of a team
And the medals and experiences led me to gleam

Change of Towns
Towards the end of year nine because of financial reasons
We had to sell our house before the Christmas season
My father had injured his back from work because of his employer
Which led my mother giving and option to me and my sister
To stay in the town for another three months but live
In a caravan, or go to Townsville to live
The option I chose was not one my mother wanted me to give
So I was forced to move with my mother and sister anyway
Despite the fact I wanted to stay

I was finally enjoying my life and achieving
But as was common in my life until then, I had to start grieving
I left the small town where I had lived most of my life
And sent to a school four times bigger, causing me strife
Apart from the size, culture and even the change
Politics happened again in my life, which sounds strange
But the administration team at the new school

Told me my A grades were only country A's and not fit for their school
So I went from top classes and achieving at worst second place
To being told by adults I was stupid to my face
They enrolled me in the lower to mid-range
So I stopped trying, and again this felt strange
I changed my focus from academic to sport
Which I felt was an acceptable thing to resort
And I quickly became good at what I chose to do
And even represented the school at the North Queensland interschool competitions too
Just when it felt politics could no long affect me again
I was beaten by one centimetre in triple jump that, measured by the competitor's teacher and friend

Changing schools meant a large cultural change for me
From the peer level to the admin team
But my difference worked favourably
As my hair cut turned about to be
Known as the "mullet" affectionally
And this allowed me make
Lots of superficial friends without my usual social ache

After being at my new school for a long time
The camara film of mine
Was sent away to be developed

And to my dismay the photograph shop could save it
All the photos I had taken were no more
And I felt terrible as I had many times before

Parent's Divorce and Parental Engagement
Most people when their parent's divorce
It causes them sadness, guilt or remorse
My parents separating was great for me
Because it meant receiving less abuse daily

Following the divorce my father slowly stopped engaging with me
And after my sister moved back with my mother and I, she
Would only see our father rarely
And I found out that during this time, my father occasionally
Would visit the house to see my sister and not me
And then after two and a half years approximately
He began communication towards me

My mother meanwhile had continued the abuse, but this slowly decreased
Whilst this was a welcome turn events, I wished it had of ceased
I had worked out that if I closed my eyes and took the hit
To my face or other body bits
The pain would decrease
And around fifteen the abuse did cease

My parents have my sister and I
That stayed together for so long, and when asked why
They said they didn't want us to live in a broken home
Whilst this intention was positive all on its own
In practice the meant for my sister and I
That there were many years' worth of reasons for me to cry
And wonder if my parents had of just said goodbye
To each other
My father and mother
Would have less need to abuse me
And I may have more years of memory

For reasons unknown to me or my wife
When I was between nineteen and twenty, my father re-entered my life
Several years into my relationship with my wife
She met my father and his new wife
My father and his partner met my first two kids
But when they moved to Melbourne his engagement did
Being to decrease
Now I am waiting for it to cease

First Love
My first "proper" romantic relationship was when I was fifteen
I was asked out by another female teen
After I cut off my "mullet" and had lost many superficial friends
Being asked out had a positive end
I was taught many behaviours of sexual nature
As my girlfriend was very sexually mature
I had never kissed a girl, and had only held hands
But during my time with her, my first sexual relationship began
I was considered by her Christian mother
To be a bad influence, and she feared I would corrupt her
But she didn't know that her "good Christian daughter"
Had for many years continue to thwart her

Eventually she dumped me for being too boring
But her social contact led to me being employed for night and morning
And I made several good friends who I knew for many years
So being broken up with, didn't end in tears

From North Queensland to Brisbane and Back
When my family moved to north Queensland and had our own rental
I returned to martial arts again, perhaps to stop me feeling mental
I was allowed to do Tae Kwon Do
And for six months I was allowed to go
I went up five belts in 2 gradings
And was beginning to do well without fading
Until my parents forced me to stop training
As a punishment, so happiness I once again stopped regaining
Years later when asked they denied
That it was a punishment but I felt they lied
Instead the official reason I was told
Was themed around finance now that I was no longer fifteen years old

In my final year of school, I went for sports age champion
And after fifty percent of the events that I was in
Was completed I was sitting in second place
Then on the final day and before the first running race
I blew my knee throwing a javelin
But I still attempted the be in
The eight hundred metre event straight after

But I was unable to walk, and there was no internal laughter
So I ended coming fourth place with no medal for me
So all I ended up with was a cool story

After graduating high school I went straight back to Brisbane
Officially it was to be enrolled in
The university program in teaching
However, many years later after reflecting
It may have been to avoid my family again
There were many positive events whilst down there
I developed my own identity and could share
My oddities without too much care
And it helped me to understand
That I need sport and mental stimulation to be the man
That I wanted to be
To allow myself to be internally happy

While back in Brisbane I returned to Karate
And in under two years I quickly
Graded to Shodan Ho and competed in
Various tournaments alone and in teams again
Where whether solo or in a team
Many medals were won, leaving my face with a gleam
I also dabbled in funk and hip-hop dance for

Assistance to James as his wingman, despite no dancing before

After attending the university in Brisbane
For less than two years, I once again
Became to focus on sport and not study
Which led to some worrying about money
So I slowly changed my focus to earning
And dropped out of university and stopped my learning

After several jobs, I eventually worked and met friends at KFC
And eventually was invited by one of the managers to a party
While downstairs playing pool with two of my female friends
When we heard a noise that in the end
Turned out to be six male gate crashers, stopping by
Who were evidently using illicit drugs to get high
And they asking for guy named John who
They were after, but we had no idea who
John was so we tried telling
Them this but they kept yelling
And after several threats from the gate crashers they luckily
Left after only throwing a pool ball at me

We eventually left the party
And we later found out the house was demolished by them
Which made me thankful for my calm decorum
Both when I spoke to the gate crashers and then my friend
Where I requested our fun at the party come to an end

Later while in Brisbane I was seeking direction
So I investigated the military option
I completed their intelligence screening test
And despite not having a couple of flying options, I had the rest
Of the job opportunities listed for me
But their quota and my age meant the recruiters wanted me for infantry
However, I decided just in time to withdraw
As I had spoken to James and his before
Which was the right decision for my brain and body
As I now know I have PTSD with serving the military

During my Brisbane time I turned eighteen
And had never tasted but had seen
Lots of different alcohol types
But never wanted to and it never felt right
To drink alcohol as I had an internal fear I would start

a fight
So thankfully on the night
That I said yes to an alcoholic beverage I was alright
James' sister encouraged consumption of a drink by me
So I drank half a glass of lemonade and Midori
To date I have had four times when I tasted alcohol
Each time having a sip or half a glass or half a bottle, never whole
As I continue to make sure I'm in control
And so I don't use substances including alcohol

Second Love
When I was at the Brisbane university
My female friends made several social media accounts for me
One day I came across a photo of one my friends
And enquired who the other person was, and in the end
I eventually asked out the person known here as Casey
Which led to positive experiences for me
I learnt a lot about relationships and how they should work
About the negatives, about communication and the many perks
Casey had many positive attributes in our relationship that I admired
And although it would end, I was mostly inspired
Eventually I made the tough decision to end it, for worse or for better
When I realised she cared more for me then I did her

Despite ending the relationship with Casey
I am grateful for the time and all the relationship taught me
After ending the relationship I soon moved back to

north Queensland
Where I lived with my mother and her partner again

Signs of My Mental Illness
The first time I realised something was not right mentally
I had my first thought of suicidality
The pain that was inside my knee
Became too much to handle mentally
I had the thought of playing chicken with the cars outside my door
But made the decision to call James before
Thankfully for me he was free that time
And he was able to get me to focus on the life that was mine
Whilst the thought would arise occasionally following this
I knew I could talk if I was feeling adrift

For as I long as could remember then
Multiple nightmares every day would happen
Where I was able to defend myself physically
Mainly against my parents who were the same size as me
As in the dream of my fifteen-year-old size
So the abuse I received as a kids would not lead to my demise
And during my sleeping state

I would also punch and kick the walls during the night
early or late

Getting to sleep was not done easily
As my thoughts were racing and my parents were
arguing about life and me
To counter the noise I would employ
The best tool I had as a teenage boy
I would listen to music to distract
Which worked very well as it did detract
From my brain and my environment

The use of the radio lessened over the years
But my nightmares continued, bringing me tears
Until I met my final love whom I am now married to
As she gave support and I started to know what to do

The same year I had the thought of playing chicken
I had a mental breakdown that made me feel stricken
I had a nightmare that included my father's dead body
Despite him still being alive and lively
I then rode to work where my boss was again late
And this triggered me because I was sick of the wait
So I quit my job, rode home and locked my door
And played some rap music turning the volume up
more
In an attempt to get rid of my emotional pain

Until my mother's partner opened the door and kept saying
To turn the music down which sent me insane
I started to cry and shake uncontrollably
And told my sister and mother who were now standing near me
That for as long as I could remember I had nightmares, where
I would retaliate to parents and attack my sister despite it not being fair
After this breakdown the nightmares lessened to only one a night
And most of the time they did not cause any fright

Another sign that my mental health was degrading
Came from the amount of martial arts training
Where I developed a reputation for being hardcore
Because I could kick and punch until my skin was raw
And even if I was in pain I would keep going
When the blood from my knuckles had begun flowing
I would also roll punch metal poles when out socially
As I thought this was normal and fine for people to see
Now looking back I understand it served a mental balm
And is known as a form of self-harm

To reinforce my need to keep up my training
An event happened that led to my emotions containing
More fear and more anger
Because of my mother's partner's brother
He threatened to burn my house down
Because he had been fooling around
With my aunty who was married at the time
And when this ended, the blame fell to the family of mine
After hearing of this threat I started carrying a knife
As the guy's family were unsavoury and I feared for my life
I told my kung fu instructor
And he informed me it was against the law
So I swapped the knife for a heavy metal pen
And felt okay again

The decision to carry a knife
When I was fearful of my life
Is another sign of PTSD
But also behaviours that were shown to me
One of my parents kept a knife under their pillow and bed
So they could sleep without dread

Realisation and Appreciation of My Sister and Improved Relationship
During my childhood and until I was nineteen
I would often start arguments and was quite mean
Towards my sister whenever a chance was there
Until one day she laid her emotions bare
I was being sarcastic and arguing too
Until she said "maybe I look up to you"
This then led to a long conversation with her
And helped me realise the amount of negative emotions I had for her
Most of which were not her fault
But was me externalising my negative emotional vault
After this conversation my relationship with my sister improved
And whilst I continue to tease her, it is far less rude

NQ Martial Arts as Self-Medication
When I returned to north Queensland from Brisbane
I returned to martial arts training once again
I dabbled in mixed martial arts and kickboxing
And eventually started Muay Thai and Wing Chun Kung Fu training
I would often train up to eighteen hours a week
And my life focus was martial arts whenever I would speak
When I met my eventual wife
My priorities changed as did my life
I began to understand that my training was for my anger
As I was once again living with my mother
And once I started to date Paige seriously
Martial arts were no longer the most important thing to me
I would continue my training attempts almost daily
Dabbling in Krav Maga, Aiki Jiu-Jitsu and Goju-ryu Karate
Until I trained for a small period in Zen Do Kai
And then dabbled again in Brazilian Jiu-Jitsu, and Aikido before saying goodbye
To my martial arts focus almost entirely
But still managed to become an instructor in health Tai Chi

I tried to casually train but after the birth of my first son
I lost my mongrel, my sparring suffered and I felt I could spar no one
I still keep up my training occasionally
But more for general knowledge and fitness, no sparring for me

More Focus on My Future Wife
While I was training at the Muay Thai location
Paige would often collect payments for people training
One day she dropped my money under the computer
To which I replied "smooth" to her
Paige would eventually initiate friendship outside the dojo with me
And eventually we started dating including going to the movies

Paige was older than I and I had a baby face
And I had brought my mother to the martial arts space
And one day the head instructor asked about my age
Who also was her brother-in-law, who then informed Paige

I would eventually ask Paige to marry me
While playing a song by 'Train' on a CD
And when I told James about my decision
He reminded me of our original conversation
Where I had planned to ask Paige after a five-year period
But if felt right to ask earlier, so I changed it

Healing Begins
As well as my focus changing
There was a positive change with my sleeping
My nightmares went from daily
To lessening around fortnightly
Alongside this my empathy
Increased my emotional language ability
Which helped my self-identity
Leading to mostly positive changes socially and professionally

Before Paige I was able to express myself with sarcasm
And now regarding my differences, I can embrace them
This had mostly positive impacts for my social relationships
However, it led to losing several long term friendships
Two in particular who were previously very close to me,
At my ten year high school reunion, they pretended to not know me
And when I later saw both of them again
They pretended to look at the ceiling or event their friend
Despite making eye contact directly with me

But now I understand and can see
That some people change for the worse and the better
And for me others' negative changes do not matter

Since meeting Paige my efforts have become more focused
And I now work on improving my life not just for me but for us
I feel that Paige's support and care
Have allowed me to lay bare
The best version of me, weird or not
And life has become easier by quite a lot

Study, Work and Mental Illness
When I as twenty I decided to study
And so I thought about things suited for me
I saw an advertisement for a personal training course
And despite the lack of money, Paige supported me once more
So after signing up I flew to Brisbane
Where my formal fitness training would begin
After the initial face-face days
I was able to fly away
Back to north Queensland and study once more
While working for my former martial arts instructor and wife's brother-in-law
I gained lots of experiences which helped me to
Become healthier, fitter and more professional too
The skills allowed me to understand the body
And would later transfer in my career in psychology

During this study time I turned twenty-one
And signs of my social difference were highlighted again
I invited eighty people to a beach volleyball party including a pool
But once again my social differences reminded me of school
Out of the eighty I had thirty yes replies

But it turned out all but one were lies
Luckily my sister's then husband invited friends he knew
And my mother, sister and Paige invited people too
The night was filled with much fun
And it taught about life lesion about levels of social connection

Around this same time Paige encouraged me to seek help professionally
So I saw a psychologist based at the university
After being referred on and several more sessions I was able
To be given PTSD and Asperger's Syndrome as my mental health labels

When my PT boss told me
That he was moving his business away from the gym at the university
I decided to stay and return to university study
I believed I liked helping people help themselves
And thought of my interests which included almost everything else
Eventually I decided on what I wanted to study
And began my four and a half year journey studying psychology
During this four and a half years I kept busy

Often working four jobs, volunteering, and even had surgery
I also married Paige, studied at TAFE and built a house which felt wild
Graduating seven months after the birth of my first child

When I was twenty-five it was confirmed
That my lack of visual ability now had a word
Known as Aphantasia, meaning no visual ability
Which helped to explain a lot of previous confusions for me
It does not affect my ability to recognise
People faces, events or other things in my life
But it means I can't see images of thinking or memories
Of the people who are the most important to me
I can't remember my wedding, or the birth of my children
But when I remember negative events I feel them
In my body as somatic changes that can
Lead to anger or negative behaviours often
Now the two labels that this is associated with are
Both of the ones I have which doesn't get me far

At twenty-seven I had a long period of dizziness
So I went to my doctor as some days I felt like a mess

And after seeing specialists
And eventually a neurologist
I had my brain scanned, and results were good
As they showed no brain damage from childhood
The neurologist labelled the experience MdDS
Which meant whilst I land, I could experience sea sickness

Family History of Mental Illness and Trauma
As well as the direct family events discussed by me
My family has a long trauma and mental illness history
Though most of my family do not believe that
Mental Illness is a legitimate impact
Both my parents had it life way harder than I've
Experienced, it is amazing that they are alive
One parent chose to be homeless from twelve to
sixteen years old
Because their parents were abusive and neglectful,
and wouldn't be told
The other was abused and put in child safety
Where they were further abused impacting them
mentally
My parents met when the youngest was sixteen
And the other was older by years thirteen
They had no positive role models for how to parent
And did the best they could, although how they went
About parenting was not great for me
I understand now they did the best they could for my
sister and me

I have approximately many relatives I have not met
Including over eight uncles and aunties, twenty plus
cousins not met yet
I have been called too black from my paternal

grandfather
And have no relationship with any grandmother
There are many possible illegitimate aunties and uncles from my maternal side
As my maternal grandfather hid information about them to protect his pride
We knew an uncle who was a family friend who was once dear
Who was in prison for my first thirteen years
I have relatives who used drugs, by the lot
And some with mental illnesses some diagnosed and some not
Most of my adult family members have been divorced multiple occasions
Not just because of mental illness, but poor boundaries and poor communication

My memory block is fortunate in many ways
As I rarely experience flashbacks now adays
If I do it is felt in my body and triggers me emotionally
Instead of being experienced visually
Unfortunately for my sister
She can remember any events that happened to her
As well as being able to remember visually
All the events she knew about that happened to me

Memory and Processing Today
My PTSD symptoms mean I have many triggers
That can cause me to perceive danger and have negative us of rigour
I need to sit in certain locations when I'm out socially
So I can feel I have control over my safety
I am great at processing information quickly
But after forty-eight hours the information can leave me
The information can be positively triggered if I see notes
That during conversation I wrote
I have constant muscle soreness from hyper-arousal
Meaning my daily tolerance for life can quickly fall
I have poor memory in general but worse with positive experiences or events
Including my wedding, and children's birth, which has meant
Conversations that would make most people happy
Often lead to me feeling poorer emotionally
Lastly I great interpersonal memory when it comes to the negative
And terrible interpersonal as discussed when it is positive

I wrote a poem called 'The Scars on my Brain'
Which I use in parenting to help explain
My negative reactions when parenting
Using the analogy of a scar that when prodded can sting

My ASD symptoms mean I sometimes misinterpret
Subtle social or emotional cues which can lead to arguments
I sometimes find it difficult to appreciate
Other's perspectives or values until it's too late
I can be very blunt or become bored quickly
When people don't challenge me intellectually

Being a Psychologist with ASD and PTSD
I have to write a lot of notes and information
When the client is in the room during a session
I have to rely on behavioural changes and consistency
Of information the clients present to me
I have developed hundreds of templates and handouts
And adapted other people's work to help clients out
Areas such as emotional experiences felt by the client
I need to use my handouts to help them, but I can be very reliant
Particular areas such as disorders of personality
I find are very difficult for me
Because of how my brain works and my memory too
I have to do more admin work then my colleagues do
I also have to work hard almost daily
To ensure my own mental health is okay enough for me to see
And help clients with their difficulties

I do have areas that I consider to be strong
Including ASD, PTSD, and ADHD, where I have rarely been wrong
And have assisted many adults to understand the length
Of their life's negative experiences and their strengths
The extra work I do for my overall health

Allows me to have the knowledge type of wealth
Regarding the interplay of exercises and brain
Which I can reword to clients and easily explain

Identifying Positive thus far
My nightmares have decreased from daily
To often better than monthly
And their content if often less negative
And about more trivial things, which I find a positive

My focus has changed from just martial art training
To focusing on my wife and children gaining
The best life I can assist them with
So I give them all I have to emotionally give

I have less mongrel and more empathy
Which is reportedly a positive, but somewhat still foreign to me
My relationship with my sister has improved
And my self-awareness continues to lead to positive outcomes and mood

I was able to partly break some negative cycle behaviours
And continue to work on any parental failures
I am the first in my family to complete high school
In one attempt, which gave the chance and tools
To then be the first to complete a certificate three
And a diploma and then a bachelor degree

I realise my parents did the best they could
And if they had a better start to life, they probably

would
And giving credit where it is due
If I ask for assistance, they often now come through
And without the support of the other positives
There is minimal chance that I would still live

Barriers only slow us down
Compared to my childhood, later life's obstacles may seem easy
But they still had an impact on me
My first New Year's Eve with Paige I was hospitalised
Working in a fridge as a butcher, then going into extreme heat was my demise
A week later was again there
From giving my shirt to Paige and leaving my chest bare
Paige's support through both events
Was positive and I told Paige what it had meant
The negative of this positive support and communication
Meant I had no negative environmental motivation
That had been used during my childhood years to
Achieve goals and maintain positive behaviours too

During my first semester of university in north Queensland
I felt some unfairness had crept in again
Because of my knee pain I required knee surgery
But the Head of Department for psychology
Felt that not being able to walk or to study
Was not a good enough reason for me to have went
And asked for a deferred date for the final assessment

At one of my jobs during my university days
I was paid in cash but tax taken from my pay
From the manager in charge of me
But when tax time came there was no record of my money
When I asked the owner where it had gone
They informed me the manager had quit after do the wrong
This led me to never trusting the word from
Any future manager in case they did me wrong

At my first psychology job things were going okay
But when the team leader left, the team was great
Despite being a young and lacking the professional wealth
We did very well working in mental health
Until the new team leader began
And tried to run a community team like the government had ran
After voicing frustrations to my supervisor and new team leader
Both told me to change careers
Luckily I did not listen
And my next psychology job helped me to professionally glisten
Eventually the company was taken over

And many of the team and the practices were metaphorically run over
Thankfully I was offered a job elsewhere
And I flourished professionally there
My next two supervisors and team leader
Were awesome and helped me to be better

Eventually I finished my professional internship as a provisional
Psychologist, completing my three thousand hours of training in all
But I took three years and one day
And AHPRA made me emotionally pay
They had changed the rules for taking too long
And when I tried to challenge this, I was told I was wrong
So on Friday I told via email
That I was deregistered, which felt like a fail
I cried in my office as I was supporting my wife and kids
But luckily great support my team leader did
She told me my position was fine
And that the role was still mine
On the Monday AHPRA told me to was a provisional psychologist provisionally
And on Tuesday AHPRA told me

I was a psychologist who was registered fully
This had a positive ending for me
But I feel in mental health especially
The main governing health body
Would provide better support professionally

My Parenting
I have already discussed how my triggers affect me
Now I feel focus on parenting mostly
There are areas of parenting I find easy
Such as answering factual life questions logically
I am also able to teach my kids most aspects of life
But leave the spiritual stuff I don't believe in, to my wife
However, perhaps the most important part
Of parenting that involves almost an emotional art
I struggle with the worse
And when triggered I become aggressive and too often curse
I have developed the poem discussed before
And developed and adapted various emotion posters
That we have on the wall
To help my kids understand emotions should they fall
However, again it is difficult for me
To put this knowledge and use the posters easily
When I can't help my kids or they ignore me
I often turn feel rejection, powerlessness and behave angrily

Despite my parental short-comings, I still feel
That my level of effort and want to improve is real
And that with a bit of luck my children will grow and

see
That they are loved and important to me
When Paige or are struggling
We can often assist each other with parenting

Moving Forward

I thought I was managing my PTSD effectively
But the stress of three children turned out to be
An indicator that I evidently
Had more work to do on myself
To improve my long term mental health
I again searched for a psychologist, but this time
I needed to find someone senior due to the
knowledge and logic of mine
I eventually found someone who used a
neurobiological approach
And after they unsuccessfully tried to use
EMDR therapy to target the previous abuse
They tried their neurological paradigm
But after several sessions the brain waves of mine
Were competing too much
So the psychologist tried another way to touch
My brain via technology
So I tried some new age approaches that were a bit
odd for me
One was bi-lateral sounds and the other a tension
release training tool
Which at first can make you feel like a fool
And in the end the most helpful tool for me
Was a program known as the "Safe and Sound
protocol" that worked for ASD and PTSD

My life motto is to "just be great"
Although used in comedy, it does cause debate
But I believe that as long as people try to be
Their best version of themselves they will see
That most things in life are achievable
And people may even achieve the unbelievable

I still have the hard work ethic I learnt from my parents' directives
And continue to develop the values of family and caring from those who were supportive
If I am working too much or spending too much time
Paige will remind me of the importance of time with the family of mine

When life got too difficult several things kept me going
Such as having a hobby, eating well and knowing
I can embrace my oddities and live a good life
With the support of friends, children and wife

Various Discriminations
When I was younger my paternal grandfather
Made me and mother
Stay outside his house because of the fact
That he and his wife thought we were too black
The fact that I was part and my mother was half Indian
Had not really impacted my life until then

The school captain event that I discussed previously had an aim
To demonstrate that I received discrimination based on my family name
As the teacher's kids did not initially
Receive leadership positions, teacher's eyes were on me
As my family were not yet considered to be locally
Accepted as we had only lived there
For less than ten years, and they thought their behaviours to be fair

Despite being given paid jobs from our rich neighbours
They still overtly and strongly favoured my sister
I was playing the trumpet at school before
My sister began playing more and more
And when I quit practice and she continued

They bought her a trumpet, and later a guitar, which I thought to be rude

Growing up I was always one of the smaller
Which had minimal negative until one particular teacher
He had an overt favouritism towards the taller
So despite my best efforts and despite peer and parent support
I received poor grades and my effort was for naught
My very tall peer who received good grades
Even challenged the grades given with no outcome change

The high school event I discussed previously
Highlighted how politics can as simple as city versus country
Being told at thirteen that my country A grades were no good
Impacted my effort and confidence and it probably should
This led to me learning about politics and its impact on life
And how context alone can cause you some strife

The last easy example if decided to discuss
Involves subtle discriminations based on income and

class
When in year ten my English subject teacher
Mocked me for using the wrong sized paper
I had completed an assessment on the only paper my family had
Which was foolscap instead of A4 so I had
To listen to the teacher explain what this was bad

I chose to only include more obvious examples
But like many there have many subtle discriminations which I feel
Would happen to most people

Memoir Close

Hopefully my attempt at basic poetry
Has still been informative and help you see
That many positives can arise
From negative experiences often to your surprise

If you are having any difficulty
There are often people or even services that will be open to see
Or to listen and help you feel better
Whether by phone, face-face or even by letter.

Appendix
The Scars on my Brain
A poem for Kids with a PTSD parent

When Daddy was little some events happened that hurt Daddy's Brain
Overtime, it mostly healed but I still feel the Pain

The pain is like a scar that you get on your Knee
Most of the time the scar is fine, and you are playful and Happy

But sometimes the scar gets bumped, prodded, or Hit
Which can cause unexpected emotions, because it hurts quite a Bit

Now when Daddy's brain scar is triggered, I feel a great deal of Pain
I may look angry, or act quite Insane
I may yell more than normal, screaming your Name
But know that Daddy still loves you, with all his body, soul and Brain

www.ingramcontent.com/pod-product-compliance
Lightning Source LLC
Chambersburg PA
CBHW051430290426
44109CB00016B/1503